# AN
# EXODUS
# THEOLOGY

At Sigtuna, Sweden, September 21, 1922

# AN

# EXODUS

# THEOLOGY

*Einar Billing*
*and the Development of*
*Modern Swedish Theology*

*by* GUSTAF WINGREN

*translated by* ERIC WAHLSTROM

## FORTRESS PRESS

PHILADELPHIA

A translation of *Einar Billing—En studie i svensk teologi före 1920* by Gustaf Wingren. Lund, Sweden: C. W. K. Gleerup, 1968.

Library of Congress Catalog Card Number 69–14616

444H68     Printed in U.S.A.     1–209

# PREFACE

This book on Einar Billing and his theological work is intended to provide non-Swedish readers with a background for some of the trends and emphases in modern Swedish theology. Swedish studies in systematic theology were not generally translated into the world languages until about the 1930's. Since the end of World War II, however, the volume of such translations has steadily increased. By that time the theological works of Einar Billing and the theological and cultural situation of his day were so far in the past that direct and unexplained translation of his work seemed inadvisable. But careful readers soon discover that the modern Swedish systematic studies, which are now available in translation, presuppose an older theological contribution by the generation of the first decades of this century. Einar Billing, in his thought and research, was without question the foremost representative of this older generation. None of his great works, however, have been translated; they remain accessible only in Swedish. Since in many respects his thought is relevant to present theological problems, it seems proper that his ideas should now be presented to an international public.

Even in Sweden, after a long period of neglect, interest in Billing's works has increased during the past decade among both the theologians and the general public. In order to present as much as possible of his own characteristic diction and thought, I have included several long quotations from his own works. The reader who is somewhat acquainted with modern

Swedish theology will readily recognize the powerful influence which Billing's thought has exercised on some of the theologians of this present generation. That influence may be even greater in the years ahead.

GUSTAF WINGREN

Lund, 1968

# CONTENTS

# CHAPTER I

# SITUATION
# AND MILIEU

### 1. Historical Criticism of the Bible

At the close of the nineteenth century historical criticism of the Bible brought about serious conflicts between the universities and the church in several European countries. This was true especially in the area of exegesis, since it was the historical study of the literary origin of the biblical texts that awakened doubts about the truth of the church's teachings. Sweden was not a pioneer in this field; quite the contrary. In several other countries professors of Old Testament exegesis were forced to resign their posts and to seek professors' chairs in other departments, as, for example, in the humanistic discipline of Semitic languages. The situation in Sweden around 1890 was rather the opposite. When Einar Billing, who was born in 1871, listened to his theological teachers in Uppsala toward the end of the century, it became obvious to him that his professors were deliberately seeking to conceal certain results of historical criticism from their wards in a well-meaning solicitude to protect their students' faith from serious crises.

These "dangerous" results were, by and large, concerned with the *Old Testament*. It was in this area that the crisis began. The New Testament writings had not yet become involved in the conflict; it is important to take note of this fact. Billing's biblical theology from 1907 on became primarily a

1

theology of the Old Testament. He viewed the uniqueness of the event of Jesus against the background of what was unique in Israel.

It was not possible, when the crisis came during Einar Billing's student years, to discover anything unique or original in the Old Testament. Skepticism had its focus at this point. Historical criticism placed the Bible in the same category as all other world literature. It seemed impossible to discover any concern or message which these books might bring to us which could not be found just as well anywhere else. This perplexity was due to the fact that the possibilities for the church of interpreting the Old Testament words in a positive sense as God's address to us were not at hand. The words had been rigidly established for centuries quite independently of any historical research and even of common, ordinary study. According to the tradition of the church, the author of the Pentateuch was Moses himself, in spite of the fact that no statement to this effect is found in any of the five books. Furthermore, Lutheran orthodoxy held to a theory of verbal inspiration, which connected God's activity primarily with the origin of the words and letters of scripture, not with the *events* which the scriptures narrate.

The shock for many of the young theologians came through Julius Wellhausen's *Prolegomena zur Geschichte Israels* (second edition, 1883).[1] What disturbed some of them, among them the student Einar Billing, was the very late date assigned to the origin of the biblical writings. The order now became quite different from what it had been hitherto. First came certain convulsive events in the history of the people (the liberation from Egypt, the march through the Red Sea and the desert, etc.). The writings and books appeared after these events and as a result of the attempts of the prophets to interpret the history of the people. The ministry of the prophets through the spoken word came prior to the writing of the Pentateuch. Far back, at the dawn of Israel's history, Moses had indeed appeared, a man who must have been a prophet and a leader of the same type as Amos, Isaiah, and the rest, but he is inaccessible to us since he did not himself produce any writings. Moses was the man at the departure from Pharaoh's country, out of the house of bondage, the man at the boisterous waves of the Red Sea. The word which later would help Israel to interpret and endure all its future vicissitudes was born in the midst of the stream of historical events.

This is the second point we should note in our introductory sketch of biblical criticism. We have already remarked that Billing's biblical theology was throughout his life a theology of the *Old Testament,* and that this was due to the exegetical situation at the time of his crisis as a student. Now we can add that his crisis was resolved through precisely this research which at first only threatened to hurt him. Wellhausen's tremendous emphasis on the sway that actions, historical events, exercised on the process of literary production furnished Billing with a starting point for a new synthesis. According to Israel's faith, God works primarily in the earthly sphere, in the surging tumult of events. Since he acts here, he also sends his word through the mouth of his prophets to help Israel interpret its history and recognize God in the turmoil. The word, too, which comes from God was considered as an *act*.[2] Billing did not develop this pattern of the dominance of the acts and events over written documents in protest against the dangerous threat to faith in Wellhausen's work. The very opposite is true. He saw the pattern grow from his study of Wellhausen and other representatives of this critical exegesis.

The pattern formed a vessel into which the contents of the New Testament could later be poured, because the situation there was exactly the same. Before a single word of the New Testament had been written, there transpired in the world a sequence of events—a man acted, went about among those possessed by demons and those laden with guilt, and, while his course moved steadily toward the cross, bestowed "forgiveness of sins" on those inmates in the house of bondage. What happened was again an exodus, an exit toward an open future, but now in a new and completely personal form. Einar Billing interpreted the work of Jesus according to the categories taken from Exodus. The New Testament writings are interpretations of Jesus' life, death, and resurrection, interpretations of the event which surpassed all other events. With this event the biblical narrative ended and the history of the church began. Consequently the task of the church is to open the way to an "exodus" for all humanity, to provide the possibility of an exit through the proclamation of the forgiveness of sins. This was perhaps Billing's most frequently expressed formula: "In the forgiveness of sins we live through our exodus from Egypt."[3] When this formula was hammered out, Billing's concept of the national church* was born, emerging directly out of his study of the Bible.[4]

After the historicocritical view had been established in exegesis, several different schools of systematic theology developed in Europe. Most of these did not appear until after 1920, after the end of World War I. Billing's conception was in all essential respects worked out before World War I began, as early as about 1911. He left his professorship at the University of Uppsala and became Bishop of Västerås in 1920. Our modern systematic theology in Sweden as well as in the whole of Europe presupposes without exception the results of

*Swedish *folkkyrka,* "folkchurch." Since this designation of the church is not current in English, I have translated *folkkyrka* as *"national* church." "National" in this context calls attention to "the people" residing in one area within the boundaries of the parish. It also applies to the whole church of Sweden thus constituted. It does not suggest the connection with the state. Wingren uses "state church" in those contexts where the connection of the Swedish church with the state is indicated. "The national church" in this translation means the Swedish church as Billing understood it: the church open to all the people, offering grace and forgiveness of sins to all within the boundaries of the territorial parish. (*Trans.*)

critical exegesis. But it is not usually the case that the fundamental structure depends on the collapse caused by biblical
criticism, on the *disintegration* of the theory of verbal inspiration, and on the ancient pattern which arose on the basis of
this collapse—*the events prior to the books*. This was Einar
Billing's specific and unique stance. For him the traditional
orthodox view of the Bible had *obscured* the real content of
the Bible. When this view was discredited, the God who acts
appeared. The biblical writings bear witness to him. Today he
speaks through their words to the nations, building his church,
still the God of history, working in his ancient element in the
course of this world, clothed in the garb of the incarnation.

In his diocesan *Pastoral Letter to the Clergy of the Diocese
of Västerås (Herdabrev till prästerskapet i Västerås stift)*, first
published in 1920, Billing himself described "the earthquake"
which rocked his mind when, in the course of his studies at
the university, he read Wellhausen's *Prolegomena*. But he also
noted the positive fruits which the earthquake bore for all his
work as a theologian:

> But when I look back it appears most remarkable that precisely
> in that same work of Wellhausen which threw me into the vortex
> of problems, and whose theses have in due order passed through
> the most severe criticism—in this work I met for the first time
> conceptions which later became the most decisive and positively
> fruitful for my entire theological and religious thinking. I did not
> notice them at that time—I saw only the negative aspect—but
> they must have lodged in my thought and germinated. If I had
> been able to listen with more composure, I might not have had to
> traverse so many byways.[5]

Since Billing regarded the work of critical exegesis as a
direct gift to the church which helps rather than hurts it, he
was disturbed at the prospect of a theological education separated from the universities. He knew from his own experience
how easily one can entertain the idea of trying to protect
oneself against health and soundness and set up barriers

against free investigation. *If* this separation between the universities and the church were to come, he maintained that for its own sake the *church* must see to it that the institutions for the training of pastors retained the atmosphere of free research which hitherto had characterized the universities.[6] For the same reason, Billing could sometimes include discussions of the results of biblical criticism in his sermons or describe those results in other contexts of worship.[7] The critical view of the Bible belongs in worship because its views and discoveries are "edifying": they promote faith and songs of praise in the congregation. This frankness, too, appears to me as something rather unique in Einar Billing's attitude.

### 2. Free Church and State Church in Sweden

Billing's first major work in biblical theology was *The Ethical Thoughts in Early Christianity (De etiska tankarna i urkristendomen)*. The first, incomplete, edition appeared in 1907. By far the largest portion was devoted to the Old Testament. His first book, however, his doctoral thesis of 1900, was concerned with Luther, not with the Bible and its books. The subject of this first production was Luther's teaching concerning the *state*. This starting point left indissoluble traces in Billing's continued work as a theologian and churchman. If one has in his early years seen from the inside how, according to the theses of the Reformation, church and state originally functioned as God's different "ways of governing," one is not so easily startled by all kinds of modern ideas regarding the true nature of Protestantism, Lutheranism, and evangelical faith. That Billing's study of Luther came prior to his work in biblical research appears to me as of rather considerable significance.

We note here one factor in Billing's situation and milieu which was typical of Sweden at the turn of the century, but which, in contrast to the widespread use of historical criticism, was not so generally prevalent in the rest of Europe. In Billing's Sweden, free church and state church stood in open conflict. Einar Billing grew up in this climate as he attended both the lower schools and the university. His study of Luther helped him in many ways to transcend the opinions that were generally and tenaciously held.

We may most easily discover Billing's typical characteristics if we consider him in the context of the free church movement at the close of the nineteenth century. Sweden was unique among the Scandinavian countries in that it was unable to retain within the national church the great flood of lay re-vivals that swept over the country about the middle of the nineteenth century. Denmark, Norway, and Finland retained these revival movements within the framework of the state churches. They did indeed receive an importation of free churches from England and the United States, as did almost all the European countries, including Sweden. But in Sweden the people affected by the revivals *turned away from* the na-tional church and Lutheran revival. This development—from the National Evangelical Foundation (Evangeliska Foster-landstiftelsen) to the Swedish Mission Covenant Church, which was founded in 1878—was peculiar to Sweden. The development was quite similar to the appearance of Meth-odism in England, where revival led away from the Church of England. There was a certain awareness of a common experience which created an affinity between the Church of England and the Church of Sweden during the first decade of our century. This affinity was quite independent of "the his-torical episcopate" and the theories connected with this office. In a peculiar sense both churches felt unrepresentative of their people.

This peculiar situation in Sweden created in a negative sense the prerequisite condition for the renewal of the national church. The impetus came from a strongly academic group of professors and other persons connected with the university. Among them were Einar Billing, Nathan Söderblom, J. A. Eklund, and Manfred Björkquist, all members of academic circles in Uppsala. Perhaps something similar can be discovered somewhere in England. But in Denmark, Finland, and Norway the state churches were trying to absorb the tremendous lay powers within their parishes. In marked contrast to their Swedish colleagues, university professors in the neighboring countries did not participate in or affect the church in the same way. Out in the parishes of these national churches were leaders with spiritual power. In Sweden, as in England, such persons tended very quickly to become leaders of independent churches.

When the Swedish national church endeavors to define itself in relation to the free churches in its midst, the pattern is almost exclusively derived from Einar Billing and his conception of the Bible. In this area, too, Billing's fundamental attitude and his stance as he approached the critical point was quite closely related to his attitude toward Wellhausen and toward historical criticism. His program was not to resist and push away, but rather to persist, accept, submit to the criticism, try to understand and penetrate beneath the surface strata of the discussion. The free churches, with P. P. Waldenström in the forefront, established the church on the basis of *received* grace, on personal faith and individual conversion. Their criticism of the national church was directed primarily against its *territorial* character, against the geographical boundaries of the parishes, and against infant baptism "without personal commitment."[8] In sharp contrast to the prevailing practice at this time, Billing constantly followed the approach of transforming these loaded, negative designations into words of honor. It is the glory of the national church that its parishes are geographical areas; it is its glory that it accepts infants as real members.[9]

When Billing attempted to prove that from a theological point of view these external forms of organization mean not weakness but rather strength, not laxity but power, he returned to the central biblical content which we described at the end of the previous section: exodus, the forgiveness of sins, this gift which the risen Christ comes bearing to nations and peoples.[10] The church must be organized in such a way that it *brings* this tendered grace to all men. It is typical that Billing conceived of the *parish church* itself as an *act,* as a *divine act,* and as a *divine act* directed to *all residents in the area.* It is directed to all these people irrespective of any religious qualifications they may possess. By this approach he placed the emphasis on that "gospel" which in Luther's theology "governed" the church in contrast to the state. The significance of this break with the old Swedish ideal of the *state* church which Billing's approach involved has not been generally recognized.[11] Drawing his support from Martin Luther and the Reformation, Billing departed from the Swedish nineteenth century and its conception of the state church, which had been represented by the so-called "great faculty" *(stora fakulteten)* in Lund and also by Billing's Hegelian-trained forebears.

We have almost forgotten that during Luther's years of crisis in Wittenberg he lived in a typically pluralistic community. Every possible confession was to be found within the city, from those faithful to the Pope to the most radical enthusiasts and iconoclasts. Luther's only weapon was the *word* he proclaimed. This word was the *gospel,* whose critical point was aimed at the legalism of both the Pope and the enthusiasts. Waldenström claimed to represent Luther and his ideas of church discipline developed in the *Deutsche Messe.* The bishops of the state church toward the close of the nineteenth century also claimed to preserve the Lutheran heritage and Luther's patriarchal conception of church and state.[12] It is

exceedingly significant in this context that Billing had the
good fortune to devote some of his most impressionable years
to a *primary* study of Luther's writings. Through this study he
was able to transcend the conflicting positions. He discovered
the function of the gospel as the "governing" word in the
church, and he saw with utmost clarity the difference between church and state.[13]

He was drawn, therefore, for theological reasons, to a study
of the *Swedish* church. At the beginning of Lutheranism in
Sweden there was an element of defiance against the earthly
kings, a trait of independence over against secular authorities.
This was an element which Billing loved. The Reformation in
Sweden was not finished until the Diet of Uppsala in 1593.
In a formal sense the enthroned king at that time was Sigismund, a Roman catholic, but actually the country was governed by Prince Carl, who leaned toward Calvinism. The
church held fast to the Lutheran confession in opposition to
two princely sovereigns, and that at a time when princes had
real authority and power. This, says Billing, is "the noblest
memory which any church retains."[14]

This reference to "the noblest memory" of the Swedish
church comes from one of Billing's most characteristic
speeches as a practical churchman, his great discourse at the
1929 Diet of the Church. In that speech he argued in favor
of the motion to allow everyone who desired to withdraw from
the state church the freedom to do so. This is a paradoxical
chapter in the later history of the Swedish church. At that
particular time the state was relatively passive toward and
uninterested in extending freedom of religion in Sweden. The
church itself took the initiative toward greater religious freedom and urged that every individual who desired to sever his
connection with the church be granted the right to do so. The
man who provided the theological arguments in favor of this
motion was the principal theologian of the national church,

the great antagonist against the free churches, Einar Billing. The arguments were derived primarily from the *gospel*. It can never become clear, he said, that the gospel is a free gift to all the people unless a consistent and radical freedom to say no is universally granted.[15] There is no question but that Billing's actions in this matter were determined by his deep anchorage in Luther's thought, in the Diet of Uppsala, and ultimately in the Bible. The church is one thing, and the state is something else.[16] God governs the world with two hands.

### NOTES TO CHAPTER I

1. This title of Wellhausen's work appeared first in the second edition (1883). The first edition (1878) had a somewhat different title. It took a relatively long time for the book to produce its decisive effect.

2. Note in this context Billing's basic analysis in *De etiska tankarna i urkristendomen* (2nd ed. enlarged; Stockholm, 1936), pp. 95 f., a passage to which we shall return later.

3. Typical passages in Billing's works are *Försoningen* (2nd ed.; Stockholm, 1921), pp. 22, 75; especially *Our Calling*, rev. trans. Conrad Bergendoff ("Facet Books – Social Ethics Series," 1; Philadelphia: Fortress Press, 1964), p. 40. Frequently the formulation is repeated verbatim, as in a liturgical text.

4. In *Kyrkosynen i Einar Billings teologi* (Stockholm, 1966), pp. 39 f., 158 f., and 190, Gösta Wrede has emphasized the connection between Billing's view of the Bible and his conception of the national church, and has cited significant passages to prove his thesis. Cf. Ragnar Ekstrom, *Gudsfolk och folkkyrka* (Lund, 1963), pp. 173–78.

5. Einar Billing, *Herdabrev till prästerskapet i Västerås stift* (2nd ed.; Stockholm, 1962), p. 48; cf. pp. 46 f.

6. See Einar Billing, *Universitet och kyrka* (Stockholm, 1923), pp. 20–22. His position is equally clear in the essay, "Den teologiska fakultetens ställning vid universiteten," *Vår lösen* (1912), pp. 305–20.

7. One example is found in Billing's posthumous collection of sermons and addresses, *Guds närhet* (2nd ed.; Stockholm, 1949), pp. 45–49, viz., a sermon delivered at St. James church in Stockholm at the annual meeting of the Swedish Bible Society in March of 1922. The genre lies between a sermon and an address, but the important point is its connection with a service of *worship*.

8. A clear view of the general situation in the debate may be obtained from the collection of essays in *Folkkyrkan och den frikyrkliga församlingsprincipen* (Uppsala, 1912), which contains contributions to a discussion held in Uppsala in 1912. Billing contributed two statements, pp. 38–57 and 98–105.

9. See, e.g., Einar Billing, *Den svenska folkkyrkan* (2nd ed.; Stockholm, 1963), pp. 50–64, 110 f., 135.

10. Cf. Einar Billing, *I katekesundervisningens tjänst* (2nd ed.; Stockholm, 1943), pp. 139–46.

11. This is very commendably emphasized in Gustaf Aulén, *Hundra års svensk kyrkodebatt* (Stockholm, 1953), pp. 41 f.

12. In regard to the claim that the Swedish free churches preserve the heritage from Luther see Bengt Hallgren, *Kyrkotuktsfrågan* (Lund, 1963), pp. 11 f., and the analysis on pp. 236–40.

13. See, e.g., Einar Billing, *Luthers lära om staten* I (Uppsala, 1900), pp. 62, 198 f.

14. *Den svenska folkkyrkan*, p. 114; cf. pp. 69–74. The same pride is evidenced in Billing's respect for his predecessor in the diocese of Västerås, Johannes Rudbeckius.

15. See in this context *ibid.*, pp. 121–26. Similar statements from Billing were repeated also when the new law of religious freedom finally was enacted in 1951. Cf. Björn Kjellin, *Lagen om religionsfrihet* (Stockholm, 1951), pp. 9–12.

16. The same distinction appears very prominently in Billing's last great lecture at the 1937 Pastoral Conference at Västerås, "Kyrka och stat i vårt land i detta nu," published posthumously as a separate book in 1942, and now inserted in its right place in the second edition of *Den svenska folkkyrkan*, pp. 128–86.

# CHAPTER II

# BILLING
# AND HIS SOURCES

## 1. The Bible

Billing's scholarly research did not go on very long: only about twenty years. That the effect of his work became so powerful and durable was due naturally to the intensity of his study, which in turn was to a large extent the result of the intensity of his own doubts and distress. But most especially the effect was due to the central objects of study he chose to pursue. The Bible and Luther gave him the themes for his scholarly production. One can hardly choose more central objects.

Chronologically, Luther was both first and last. Luther was the subject of Billing's doctoral thesis of 1900, and also of his last scholarly work, published toward the end of his professorship. The title of the latter work was "1517–1521"; it was a contribution to the study of Luther's development, published for the 1917 quadricentennial of the Reformation. But it is no exaggeration to say that while he wrote about Luther he was continually thinking about the Bible. This orientation was really quite inevitable. One does not find anywhere in the history of Western culture a voluminous literary production as entirely and naïvely subservient to the Bible as Luther's. Almost every page is simple and faithful interpretation of the Bible.

Billing's principal work was devoted to the interpretation of the Bible. *The Ethical Thoughts in Early Christianity (De etiska tankarna i urkristendomen)* was published in 1907, followed in 1908 by *The Atonement (Försoningen).* In size and form this latter work is rather modest, but it is nevertheless a prime example of genuine scholarship. We should note well that at all times Billing dealt directly with the original Hebrew and Greek texts. In problems of biblical theology Billing did not base his judgments on translations. References to the original text frequently appear unobtrusively in passing, even in sermons and extemporaneous speeches. In this introductory chapter to Billing's theology we shall ignore for the present all problems, and deal only with certain features in the general situation of scholarly research in which Billing did his work.

In Billing's time the interpretation of the Old Testament moved in the areas of history of religion and literary criticism. Both of these disciplines tended to dissolve the biblical material and transform it into something else. The material was broken up into sections paralleling other religions, or into "primary sources." These were conceived of quite pedantically as smaller texts, older than the present biblical books. In contrast, the cult was mostly ignored. The scholarly gains in this period were found in the continuing comparison of Israel with the surrounding cultures of Babylonia, Assyria, and Persia. This provided in reality excellent means for discovering what the *specific* element in the Old Testament really was. Billing remained within the problem areas of the history of religion and literary criticism, but he used these areas as means in his work.[1]

He also added other means which were not as generally used at that time. He compared Israel's prophets with the Greek philosophers, for whom external history, which in the Old Testament was God's proper element, played no signifi-

Th1000

cant part. The Greeks rather regarded the events and changes in the world as disturbing elements in the thoughts of the wise. Israel's conception of the divine, of that which really "is," must have originated under conditions quite different from those prevalent in Greece.[2] But Billing went further and discussed in a very original manner the problem of Judaism and its inability to discover God's actions in history and in the vicissitudes of the people.[3]

On the basis of this Jewish orientation Billing saw the New Testament in a new light. What was new in Jesus' teaching was the application of the concept of election to the *individual*. What God gave to his own people through the liberation from Egypt, that he gives through Christ to the individual: exodus through forgiveness. In Billing's time New Testament interpreters had not yet given up the attempt to write a life of Jesus. To some extent Billing remained in this biographical orientation. This is particularly obvious in his interpretation of the relationship between John the Baptist and Jesus.[4] Because of his emphasis on the individual, the early Christian conception of the church played a less significant role for him than it does in modern interpretation of the New Testament. Nevertheless Billing's unique conception of the church is directly related to his emphasis on the individual. The risen Christ searches for all individuals in the whole world, and this search is the essence of the national church.[5]

In his constant concern for the individual and his conscience, Billing appears progressive and ahead of his time. This concern was an element in Billing's conception of the church which since his time has not received sufficient attention. His interpretation of the New Testament (1907) and his motion about "free withdrawal from the church" (1929), in spite of their dissimilarity, point toward a goal not very closely related to collectivism.

**2. Luther and the Reformation in Sweden**

Billing was the pioneer of the Scandinavian Luther renaissance. About 1900 Karl Holl was known principally as a patristic scholar; at that time he had not yet begun his historical studies of the Reformation. Many regarded Luther as essentially the originator of Lutheranism, and this view was held at that time even by many experts in the field. The discontinuity between Luther and Lutheranism was unrecognized both by historical scholars and by the church. Luther was therefore incorporated into the Lutheran confessions, where he stood together with Melanchthon and the Formula of Concord.

When we consider the general effect of modern Reformation research, the most important result has been that the *universality* of Luther now appears clearly. Many factors besides research have contributed to this new conception of Luther. The dialectic theology has created a remarkable renewal in the Reformed communions, and in doing so has quoted Luther as theological authority more frequently than it has Calvin and Zwingli. This is one of the factors that have moved Luther's voice out from the closed circle of the Lutheran confession. During these later years we have in addition heard Luther speak in Rome at the Second Vatican Council, and here, too, it seems that the dialectic theology has been the intermediary agent. But even simple and commonplace results from rather pedestrian research at the universities, conducted without any intention of changing the churches, have contributed to the new appreciation of Luther's universality. Among them we may mention the patient delineation of differences between Luther and Melanchthon, between Luther and the Formula of Concord, and between Luther and the great Lutheran theological systems of the seventeenth century. In this work many individual university theologians from various countries have taken part. Einar Billing belongs among these, but in a very special sense.

As soon as we consider Luther in connection with the problems of *biblical interpretation,* he appears at a point where he functions *in a universal sense.* All churches interpret the Bible and seek to discover its central meaning. When we turn our attention to Luther's attempts to open up the Bible, we automatically permit Luther to participate in that conversation which all the churches everywhere carry on with one another in the presence of contemporary listeners. This was what Billing did. And so did Söderblom and a number of Swedish theologians of the next generation, especially in Lund since the days of Aulén and Nygren.[6] In this context one should not underestimate the practical part which participation in the international ecumenical movement played. Both Billing and Söderblom participated early in the ecumenical dialogue, the latter as one of the leaders.[7] The following generation of Swedish theologians, again especially in Lund, has as a rule both occupied itself with Luther and participated in the ecumenical conversations without sensing any insoluble conflict between these two tasks. When we read Luther, we hear a man from the sixteenth century speak in the pluralistic setting of Wittenberg—and he spoke to the *whole* of Christendom: to the Pope, to the enthusiasts, to his companions in faith, and to anyone who wanted to listen.

This sketch is historically accurate, because Luther's real milieu was diversified and un-Lutheran. But this fact makes Luther also remarkably relevant—it is as though he were now speaking to the twentieth century. What is irrelevant is the Lutheranism which through governmental legislation became curtailed, protected, and isolated. *That* no longer exists. Personally, I believe that new possibilities for discovering the true Luther in contrast to the succeeding confessional Lutheranism depend to some extent on the pluralistic situation of the twentieth century. This pluralistic situation grew out of the legislation establishing religious liberty, the sudden growth of communications, and the resultant disappearance of the

fences that separated people from one another. Einar Billing's
way of thinking emerged in the midst of the birth pangs of
this new age. Earlier than others, he saw what was coming.
The paradoxical fact that he was the theologian par excellence
of the national church and still *demanded* from the as yet
passive Swedish state that individuals be given the right to
withdraw freely from that church—this fact is really not paradoxical at all, but simple, logical reasoning.[8] As long as the
church possesses other powers besides *the word of the gospel,*
it is weak, decrepit, and perplexed.

We have already emphasized the significance of the fact
that it was Luther's teaching about the state, and in particular
his concept of the *difference* between "the two realms," that
constituted the starting point for Einar Billing's study of
Luther. This study preceded his work in biblical theology.[9] As
a result Billing's attention was directed to the same problems
in the sixteenth century debate which he himself faced in the
twentieth century discussion. In both instances it was the
unique nature of the church over against the state that was
the chief problem.

In this context we note that Billing followed a selective
principle in relation to later Swedish Lutheranism also. He
went forward from the beginning, about the year 1520, both
in Germany and Sweden, but he did not go on to the specific
doctrines of seventeenth century Lutheran orthodoxy. He did
not accept the satisfaction theory of the atonement, the theory
of the inspiration of the Bible, etc. On the contrary, he
rejected these mildly and reasonably when he sometimes
mentioned them.[10] What Billing positively took up in the subsequent Lutheranism, especially in Sweden, and what he there
emphasized was the fearless assertion by Lutheran churchmen
of the freedom of the church in relation to the state. Olaus
Petri, Laurentius Petri, the men present at the Diet of Uppsala
in 1593, Johannes Rudbeckius—all of these are mentioned by

Billing as men who were given the task of defending the gospel against interference and coercion by the state.[11] If in their day they fulfilled any other functions, it is obvious that Billing regarded these as minor and uninteresting.

This aspect of Swedish church history reappeared in Billing's guest lecture at Königsberg University in 1927 on the subject of Sweden's position in evangelical Christianity. The speech was published in 1930 in *The Swedish National Church (Den svenska folkkyrkan).*[12] In his speech at the 1929 Diet of the Church, published in the same volume, Billing reviewed the history of the church and somewhat narrowly emphasized the same point.[13] This was evidently a matter which he felt should frequently be repeated.

### 3. A Brief Biographical Sketch

Sweden is, to be sure, a small country, but it is impressive in length. There is a considerable difference in the cultural climate between the south and the north. Einar Billing's father, Gottfrid Billing, had his roots in the south, in Skåne, where his proper place was the episcopal see of Lund. To this office he was elected in 1898. Prior to this move he had been Bishop of Västerås (1884–98). He had therefore held the same episcopal office to which his son Einar was elected in 1920. Einar Billing's early years were inextricably intertwined with his father's career.

Einar Billing was born in Lund on October 6, 1871, while his father was professor there. He lived in Lund as a boy long enough to acquire the peculiar dialect of Skåne, which later on in Uppsala created a somewhat foreign impression that always remained with him in the milieu of central Sweden. But in 1884, when he was thirteen years of age, he moved to Västerås and lived in the same bishop's residence where he was to live later in life, and where he also was to die. Västerås is in a sense an "all-Swedish" diocese. Here have occurred significant events in the history of Sweden, in which men from the province of Dalarna have frequently participated. Einar Billing loved Dalarna and became firmly attached to this north central part of Sweden. As a student he naturally attended the University of Uppsala, not Lund. He frequently visited Lund and was ordained there in the cathedral, but there, too, he was regarded as a stranger—as a person from the north. Billing thus transcended the loyalty demands of the two rival university communities, Uppsala and Lund, and was therefore protected from many elements of personal provincialism.

During the years 1889–1900 he was a student at Uppsala. He concluded his studies with his doctoral dissertation, *Luther's Teaching Concerning the State (Luthers lära om staten)*. He became at once lecturer (docent) at Uppsala, thus beginning an academic career that lasted two decades, from 1900 to 1920. In the year 1908 he became assistant professor and the following year, full professor. His whole professorial career was spent at Uppsala. It was interrupted by a few brief trips to foreign universities, mostly German. Honorary doctorates were conferred upon him by the universities in Greifswald and Marburg.

During his time as professor the old arrangement that a theological professor served also as a pastor of a parish was still in force. Billing was chief pastor *(kyrkoherde)* in two parishes in the archdiocese of Uppsala: first in Hagby and Ramsta until 1918, and during the last two years at Holy Trinity in Uppsala. He left the university in 1920 and became Bishop of the Diocese of Västerås.

Theologically Billing produced nothing *new* after 1920. His theology must be characterized as "Swedish theology before 1920." But many of the implications of his theology on the practical and congregational level were developed after 1920. He did this particularly in the Diet of the Church, where he played a very significant role as a member of the Committee on Church Law. During the last few years before his death in 1939, his influence began to wane. This was due partly to failing health and partly to new movements within the church. He died on December 17, 1939, after he had with a tremendous effort officiated at an act of ordination.

It may seem that his career was not of great significance. He made hardly a move that was not predetermined by his paternal home and its circumstances. But his greatness lay on an inner plane. His father, Gottfrid Billing, was a central figure in Swedish political life and one of the dominant men in the Swedish parliament; yet he never sought to hide the fact that theologically and spiritually he received instruction from his son Einar, even in early years.

In the circle of "young churchmen" in Uppsala from 1908 on—men who became significant for modern Swedish church history—there were many who were more active and enterprising than Einar Billing. But there was none whose moral authority was recognized by the others to such a high degree, and whose judgment on proposed projects was more respected. When a new idea was proposed, they asked spontaneously what Billing would think about it. If he assented, the hesitation vanished.[14] During the time he was a bishop, he often held the same position among his peers in the Swedish church as a whole. It is characteristic that in 1922 he was the real author of the answer from the Bishops' Conference to the Anglicans in regard to intercommunion. However, three other —older—bishops signed the document. Among them were Söderblom and Gottfrid Billing, who were members of the commission.[15] In a very real sense Einar Billing's work was done without personal publicity.

In his personal life he tended toward self-examination and vexation of spirit. At certain times he was subject to deep depressions, like many others who have given certainty and strength to their fellowmen.[16] His hymn, "Now rejoice, my spirit, in the Lord," in the *Swedish Psalmbook* (No. 380 in the edition of 1937) deals characteristically with joy and confidence, but the hymnist himself did not have what he sang about. Instead he cried out a divine command to his own heart, a command to cast out despair: "Let sorrow and anguish yield at the bidding of God the Almighty." His words about "the burning region of sorrow" reveal personal experience. They were not a cliché.[17]

In one sense Einar Billing at last came home to Lund, the city of his birth. His manuscripts, letters, and other remaining papers were brought to the University Library at Lund in 1966. Here also the archives of his father, Gottfrid Billing, have been preserved. During all his years Einar Billing corresponded regularly with his parents, usually once a week.[18] These "Lund letters" from both sides are now assembled, together with other manuscripts, in Lund.

### NOTES TO CHAPTER II

1. See, e.g., Einar Billing, *De etiska tankarna i urkristendomen* (2nd ed. enlarged; Stockholm, 1936), pp. 123–34.

2. *Ibid.*, pp. 9–76. At several points in his later description of prophetism Billing returns to comparative analyses in which he utilizes the results from his survey of the history of Greek philosophy (e.g., *ibid.*, pp. 102–8, 122, 150, and elsewhere).

3. *Ibid.*, pp. 188–220; also, Einar Billing, *Försoningen* (2nd ed.; Stockholm, 1921), pp. 41–59. In this context 2 Esdras becomes a central figure to which Billing again and again returns.

4. Most beautifully perhaps in *De etiska tankarna*, pp. 354–58, 406–9.

5. See *Försoningen*, pp. 94–120. The theme recurs in his work on the catechism and in his *Pastoral Letter*.

6. Cf. Gustaf Aulén, "Lundensisk teologisk tradition," *Svensk teologisk kvartalskrift* (1954), pp. 241 f.

7. See the relevant notes in Gösta Wrede, *Kyrkosynen i Einar Billings teologi* (Stockholm, 1966), pp. 167, 152.

8. The central place of the *individual* in Billing's interpretation of

the New Testament naturally constitutes the deepest and most unifying element in his line of thought. But Luther also plays a part. Cf. Wrede, *op. cit.,* p. 92.

9. Billing wrote two monographs on Luther: *Luthers lära om staten* (1900), and "1517–1521. Ett bidrag till frågan om Luthers religiösa och teologiska utvecklingsgång," *Uppsala universitets årsskrift* (1917). The first one is unquestionably of greater importance.

10. Einar Billing, *I katekesundervisningens tjänst* (2nd ed.; Stockholm, 1943), p. 100; and *Herdabrev till prästerskapet i Västerås stift* (2nd ed.; Stockholm, 1962), pp. 43–56.

11. Einar Billing, *Den svenska folkkyrkan* (2nd ed.; Stockholm, 1963), pp. 70–85. Through his own research Billing was well acquainted with Rudbeckius, as is evident from his learned essay on "Johannes Rudbeckius' aristotelism" in *Från Johannes Rudbeckius' stift* (1923), pp. 91–146.

12. *Den svenska folkkyrkan,* pp. 65–103; also published in German in *Auslandsstudien* (Königsberg, 1928).

13. *Ibid.,* p. 114. We should also mention the sermon which Billing preached in Västerås at the commemoration of the Reformation in 1927 on the subject, "A Sower Went Out To Sow" (*Guds närhet* [2nd ed.; Stockholm, 1949], pp. 32–36). From the king and the government he demanded just one thing: *freedom* for the word of the gospel.

14. See Manfred Björkquist, "Einar Billing och ungkyrkorörelsen," *Einar Billing in memoriam* (Stockholm, 1940), p. 87.

15. The information that Einar Billing was the author was supplied to me in a private letter from Archbishop Yngve Brilioth dated May 21, 1954. (Brilioth had intimate personal knowledge of the ecumenical situation prior to the "Life and Work" conference in Stockholm in 1925). Cf. also C. H. Lyttkens and V. Vajta (eds.), *Church in Fellowship* ([Minneapolis: Augsburg Publishing Concern, 1965], pp. 181–88), which does not contain any reference to any sources. (Nor do the minutes of the Bishops' Conference record who was the author.) As a matter of fact, even in the year 1909 Billing prepared the agenda for the discussion with the Anglicans during that year. Anyone who knows the theology of that period recognizes Billing's typical diction in the formulations. No one else spoke in just that fashion. See, e.g., the statements about the pastoral office in *Kyrkohistorisk årsskrift* 23 (1923), pp. 367–69 (Letter to the Anglicans, 1922).

16. Cf. Einar Billing, *De heligas gemenskap* (Uppsala, 1911), pp. 23 f. and 35–42, where he himself speaks of suffering as a service to others who suffer.

17. Cf. Oscar Krook, "Einar Billing som religiös personlighet," *Einar Billing in memoriam,* p. 192.

18. See Gerda Billing, *Fjärran Upsalaår* (Stockholm, 1955), pp. 5, 11, *et passim.*

# CHAPTER III

# ISRAEL
# AND HISTORY

## 1. Greece and the Prophets

According to Billing, "intellectualism" constituted the most obvious limitation of Greek philosophy. Every intellectualistic ethics must of necessity leave great crowds of people behind on the road.[1] But this limitation was only quantitative. It affected only the number of people who could be reached by the ethical discourse. The limitation in respect to the individual and his inner life was of much greater consequence. Within the individual's inner core there was "no struggle that had to be won, no impurity that must be cleansed away."[2] The problem was limited to the questions how "reason" could attain to the knowledge of the good and how this same reason could afterward guide the person and his actions. Within reason itself nothing new happened, nothing was *created*. Within it there were no contradictions, no "crises."

The situation in Israel was quite different. There the voice of God awakened a crisis in man's inner core, in "the heart." The good was continually given in what God spoke and in the new that he caused to appear. The field where the good was realized was in one's relationship to one's neighbor, in purely commonplace and everyday chores. In this field the actions of *all* had the same scope, and here, therefore, "the people," the many, played just as central a part as "the wise."

There were no exclusively *wise men* to be found. No one in Israel was engaged in improving himself, or in developing the self. If an individual manifested some "virtues," they were by-products of the process in which every individual was broken and reborn when God spoke in his heart. This process took place while the individual performed the most simple, common, everyday duties. This Israelite structure appeared as early as the Decalogue, with its introductory statement concerning the deliverance out of Egypt (Exod. 20:2; Deut. 5:6) and with its list of completely elementary commandments. Billing came to the Decalogue after he had summarized the aristocratic intellectualism of Greek philosophy. He wrote:

> A stronger sense of contrast can hardly be found in all the history of ethics than that which appears when we confront the conceptions whose development we have now followed with the document in which all the ethical ideas of the old Israel have received their most pregnant and classical codification—the Decalogue (Exod. 20:1–17; Deut. 5:6–21). What was absent in Hellenism is found here, and what was found in Hellenism is here absent. Here is a God whom men need not first seek in a distant metaphysical beyond. On the contrary, he himself comes into the midst of man's life, a God who is, one might say, almost too near to man. Man cannot escape from him. Whether he looks forward or toward the past, man encounters evidences of his power. . . . The relationship to him must be uppermost in man's mind. Even a casual look at the Decalogue shows us that this conception of God embodies a strong ethical compulsion. This God is not satisfied with external acts. He takes command also of the inner life: "You shall not covet. . . ." The first question is not what becomes of man himself, but how God's will is respected and again, how his people will fare. In the presence of his commands, all criticism must keep silence. No one has the right to inquire about the reasons for his will. It is enough to know that he wills it. The order is obvious. First the individual's duties in regard to God himself, then those due to father and mother, the small family unit, and finally that order of justice on which the existence of the people rests. There is nothing said about man's duties toward himself. There seems to be no room for the chief ideal of Hellenism: the development of the individual self.[3]

Since the source out of which the ethical propositions flowed was, on the Greek side, the discovery of the *concept,* that which is indifferent to history, that which stands above all change, and that which "truly is," and since in Israel the source of the commandments was an external, historical *event,* the deliverance out of Egypt, Billing could summarize Israel's peculiar individuality in the following words:

> The process of self-appraisal through which the new ethical insights appeared took place in the confrontation with God's acts in history. If we wanted to accentuate the difference we might say that what the discovery of the cognitive value of the concept meant for the Greeks, that was what the passing through the waves of the Red Sea meant for Israel's ethical thinking.[4]

It was not simply that historical events just happened to produce Israel's ethical thinking so that later the people, without returning to the history, could carry with them "the thoughts" in their mind. The thoughts remained only in a continuing reflection on the history. They were "condensed history."[5]

This unceasing return to what actually happened—in memory, in the narrative of the Exodus at the celebration of the Passover, in the cult—filled the ethical commandments with a very definite content. What God did for Israel in the Exodus was *an act of judgment* "through which God secured justice for his unjustly oppressed people."[6] To care for the weak and the oppressed was to "secure justice," that is, actively to secure the establishment of justice and the destruction of injustice. This is what the one who is merciful does. He does not let go until the oppressed have obtained justice. Righteousness itself is mercy, as the ideal judge was described, for example, in the figure of the servant of the Lord in Isaiah 42:1–4.[7] Such a unity of righteousness and mercy grew out of remembrance of the life in Egypt and the deliverance from that bondage. When in later Judaism this remembrance faded, and God's acts in history began to seem faraway, then the unity of righteousness and mercy was lost. Then righteousness degraded into retribution, and mercy degenerated into indulgence. The former condemned; the latter softened the judgment.[8] When the history faded, the commandments emerged mechanically out of the paragraphs of the code. In contrast, however, when the history was alive, one experienced the power of Exodus in *the present*. Then the ethical demands flashed like lightning directly out of the event. Then even the demands of the law were condensed history.

> Even when the law penetrated most deeply into community affairs, it still rested on a religious foundation. One notices how the thought goes back of itself, spontaneously and inadvertently, to the religious sphere and there finds its point of orientation. If we ask why, the law gives the same answer as the prophets did previously. When the lawgiver tried to make every Israelite conscious of his solidarity with every one of his brothers, and likewise when he spoke for the stranger, he looked back again and again to the wonderful events through which God had made Israel a people and had given them their land. *They could discover their duties on the basis of their historical experiences.* "You shall not oppress a stranger; you know the heart of a stranger, for you were strangers in the land of Egypt" (Exod. 23:9). "You shall remember that you were a slave in Egypt, and the Lord your God redeemed you" (Deut. 15:15; cf. Exod. 22:21 ff.).[9]

Billing's observations regarding Israel were reinforced by a comparison with Greek thought. The events from which Israel derived its ethical commandments and the power to obey them were to an outside observer just as commonplace, political, and military in their nature as the historical events through which Athens was saved from the Persians. One cannot even imagine that Socrates or Plato could have derived any pregnant ethical regulations directly from the battles of Marathon or Salamis.[10] But Babylon, Assyria, and Egypt received mention again and again in the proclamations of the prophets. The rumblings of history disturbed the ethics of the wise men in Greece; the philosopher must learn how to separate himself from this realm of flux and instability. But

the very opposite was true of Israel's leaders. When they
entered the tumult and fluctuations of history, out there in
"the thunder of many peoples" (Isa. 17:12), they met *their
God,* who alone *is* and who never fails.[11] The deeper the
prophet entered into history, the closer he came to his true and
spiritual element.

Consequently, all duties in Israel were social. The prophets
summarized their whole criticism of the morality of the people
in *one single* accusation: the lowly and the helpless among
God's people were treated unjustly. All ethical interest focused
ultimately on how "the judgment seat in the gate" functioned.
This is a matter which we are apt to classify as a social, rather
than, technically speaking, an ethical problem.[12]

An individualistic ethics was, strictly speaking, not found
in Israel, if we mean by this a system of regulations for the
care and growth of one's own personality. (This was undoubtedly the chief interest of the Greeks in their formulation of an
ethos.)

If now we turn our attention to Babylon and to the Code
of Hammurabi and make a comparison, we find the same
situation as in the case of the Greeks. What the law of
Hammurabi wanted to preserve was the individual's right to
the possession of property. In Israel, on the contrary, the
right to one's own possessions was circumscribed, for example,
by the rule about common harvest (Deut. 23:24 f., 24:19 ff.),
by the regulations for the sabbatical year (Deut. 15:1 ff.),
and by those for the year of Jubilee (Lev. 25:8 ff.). It is not
an exaggeration to say that the principle of private property
was unknown in Israel. The justice due to the neighbor, and in
Israel this meant justice for the *poor,* was the center of Israelite
ethics. This meant that the encroachment of the poor on one's
private property was *righteousness.*[13]

Egypt and the Red Sea had their influence on all this
thinking. In a public act God had interceded for the one who

was lowly and helpless. His righteousness, which is identical with mercy, demanded inexorably active concern for "the stranger, the orphan, and the widow" (Exod. 22:21–24; Deut. 10:18, 24:17–19)—always this trilogy.[14] The certainty of a future for all the peoples of the world arose on the basis of the experience in Egypt and the social demands derived from it. God, who performed the miracle in Egypt, can never cease to be what he is. He will always take care of the one who is unjustly oppressed, and he will raise the poor from the dust (Ps. 113:7). If Israel will not obey his commandments, he will go along without it. He is not tied down to the existence of his own people. Again we must note that this certainty, which was unusual in the Orient, grew out of the soil of these events, the exodus out of Egypt and the return from the Exile.[15] In neither case did Israel possess any strength in itself, but the rescue came each time because God governed the tumultuous peoples.[16] He would always remain what he was. The certainty of a *goal* in history was lacking among the Greeks. They knew only "an endless cyclical return."[17] This certainty of Israel, held fast in faith and nurtured by external, historical events repetitiously narrated, has proceeded from Israel to the Christian congregation, and from there it has entered into the world view of Western culture.[18]

When righteousness and mercy were thus radically conceived as a unity, the demand became at once both simple and infinite. Man could never escape it. But when the claim of righteousness became legalized to such an extent that one could keep it by giving every man his exact due, one could quickly be done with it. Then there was plenty of room for an extra compassionate goodness, that is, for charity. But in that case mercy became something other than righteousness, and then one had in reality lost contact with Israel's faith.[19] But in another sense the terse commandments of the original, prophetic Israel are infinite. No sector of life stands outside and apart from the light of faith. There is no profane area of existence. Just as God is actively present in the tumult and thunder of the peoples, so man as he acts is closer to his God-given, ethical field of operation when he penetrates most deeply into the everyday life and suffering of the world. There in the depths dwells poverty, and there the poor can be raised from the dust, and there the work of righteousness can be done.[20] This is the root of the well-known fact that Israel always showed respect for ordinary work with the hands. Such respect was unknown among the Greeks.[21]

Billing derived these features of Israel's ethos from its view of history, not primarily from the doctrine of creation. It would, however, have been just as possible to start in Genesis as in Exodus. It makes little difference where one starts, just so the whole content of Israel's faith is kept in view. The narrative of creation in Genesis has its center in the story of man. Man's life and preservation from death, that is, his "salvation," is the central idea in everything that is said. The story of the departure out of Egypt reveals—in passing, as something obvious—that of course Yahweh is Lord over Pharaoh, over the toads and the grasshoppers, over darkness and sickness, over the winds and the waves of the Red Sea. He is the Creator in whose hands the world rests.[22] Genesis has its Exodus element, and Exodus has its Genesis element, a fact which Billing noted quite clearly. But sometimes his reasoning faltered. He devoted years to reflection on the significance of the historical events for the development of Israel's specific faith. But in contrast he did not himself explore the fact that Israel's God, according to Israel's faith, had created all things and all beings, so that nature itself, apart from the teaching of the prophets, bore witness to God. This aspect of the doctrine of creation is wanting in Billing's theology. This lacuna brings his thought into near affinity with the continental theology which arose after 1920.

After Billing had interpreted Israel's law as milder and more humane than Hammurabi's, he continued his exposition:

> In all our discussion so far we have nevertheless followed only one of the directions which have revealed the influence of Israel's religious faith on the conception of justice. Side by side with the greater leniency which marks its law in contrast to that of Hammurabi, there is also just as characteristically a greater severity. We encounter this severity at those points where infractions of the law take on the character of *perversity*. At several different points there appears in Israel's law a reverence for what is *natural*, a fear of disturbing any of the boundaries which *life itself* has established. This feature is totally absent from the Babylonian law.[23]

Billing cited several examples: the rules against tattooing, mutilation, sexuality in the cult, etc. But most interesting in this quote is the modern Western formulation: "the boundaries which life itself has established." The Old Testament does not say that "life" establishes any boundaries. Such language belongs to the modern Westerner, for whom the world is devoid of any divine activity. But the same Westerner would also say about the *historical* events in Israel's past that "the course of this world," or "the succession of events," or something else, provided deliverance for the people from many dire circumstances. Billing avoided the Western usage at the latter point, in respect to history. In nature, however, he could see only "life itself" providing form and substance. And this in spite of the fact that the Book of Job stands there in the Old Testament with its mighty picture of God's activity in creation. (The narrative of creation in Genesis appears really as a pale reflection of Job, the Psalms, and Deutero-Isaiah.)[24] Here we see how Wellhausen's critique of the Pentateuch had influenced Billing and to some extent narrowed his view. The accent was allowed to fall on the deliverance from Egypt and on the ethical effects of this event: the care of the weak and the unjustly oppressed. From the point of view of the doctrine of creation one could say that oppression of the weak is

destruction of creation, that selfishness is unnatural, and that
the just act of judgment that raises the lowly out of the dust
is restoration of creation. But we can find no such formulations
in Billing.[25]

On the other hand, it was due to this lacuna, the minor
place of creation in his thought, that history really received
the emphasis. Something that had happened in ordinary history—the Exodus—became the spring from which flowed both
the biblical confidence for the future, that is, the eschatological
hope, and the biblical tranquility in regard to the course of
the world, that is, the doctrine of creation. Faith continually
receives strength from this event. When the doctrine of creation becomes a separate doctrine, it easily becomes doctrinaire
and without historical context, as is clear from much
*Schöpfungstheologie* of the 1930's. Billing was remarkably
free from this tendency, even though his use of the term
"people" *(folk)* could have led him in that direction. He used
this term in the important conception of "the national *(folk)*
church." But he rejected sharply and decisively the ideas
about "the people" which characterized the Deutsche Christen
movement after 1933. He did this as early as his speech at
the Pastoral Conference in Västerås in 1937.[26] Billing subor-
dinated the doctrine of creation to faith in the God who acts
in *history*.[27] He carried out a similar subordination of every
other theme to the theme of history with exceptional consistency. This process of thought appears perhaps most clearly in
his explanation of what God's revelation in "word" meant for
the prophet's own consciousness.

Anyone who searches for biblical support for the doctrine
of verbal inspiration generally isolates such Old Testament
passages as those which state that a word has been given to
the prophet: "a word sounds in his ears" (cf., for example,
Isa. 5:9 and 22:14). Here, it would seem, is a special revelation
in a *word* from God which is not connected with historical

events. But Billing demonstrated convincingly that these words were altogether *sending* words, words which dispatched the prophet to a given task, and precisely to a task in the life of *the people*. The word in the heart of the prophet was a deed of God in history. It gave to Israel the interpretation of the external, naked historical sequence. This interpretation had to be supplied if the people were really to be guided through the turbulence of the events.[28] The original type was obviously Moses, who stood in the midst of the events and who at the same time received *words* from Yahweh which interpreted the events. Only then did the whole event become an *exodus* out of Egypt. God acted toward Israel along two lines at the same time.

> His ingression into the history of his people went along on two lines: one followed the external course of events; the other was parallel to it in the consciousness of the prophets. The overwhelming power which expressed itself in historical events, in the great historical catastrophes, was the same power which operated in the consciousness of the prophet, and which compelled him to abject submission.[29]

Billing used as examples Amos and Jeremiah, who *must* go and proclaim the word (Amos 3:7 f.; Jer. 1:7, 9), and thus bring about "the breaking down" and "the building up."[30] The Old Testament describes the word itself as an action. It is therefore not merely a pronouncement, but a creative word out of which something new appears.

The same pattern appeared when Jesus in the fullness of time contemplated his own new task. "All things have been delivered to me by my Father." No other saying of Jesus appears more often in Billing's exposition of what the new act given to the Son meant. He called the passage Matthew 11:25 ff. "the great word," "the only place in the Synoptics where Jesus speaks freely of his relationship to the Father and of the revelation which he had received from him."[31] What had been given in Jesus' consciousness as a revelation from

God was a *task*: forgiveness of sins to those "who labor and
are heavy laden" (Matt. 11:28). This was the task for which
he had been *sent*. What those who were heavy laden received
from him was exodus, liberation.[32] Here in Jesus' proclamation
*nature*—sun and rain (Matt. 5:45)—began finally to speak
the same language as *history* in the Old Testament. It was the
language of mercy and of the Father's love. Consequently the
ethical demand in its highest form, love of enemies, followed
immediately and directly from God's activity in nature itself,
from the sunshine and the rain on the evil and on the good.
"Love your enemies and pray for those who persecute you"
(Matt. 5:44).[33] Jesus was not like the prophets sent to carry
on God's work among only one people, Israel. He was sent to
do God's work with every individual:

> Here, in respect to the individual, he found no point of contact
> in history. Nature took the place of history. . . . We see clearly
> that this was his way of thinking when we note how ethical
> demands sprang directly out of his conception of nature. . . . In
> other words, the conception of nature had in this context exactly
> the same ethical effect as history. It released the same moral
> energy as the events through which God visited his people. If we
> are not mistaken, this was something new. The explanation is
> found in the fact that for Jesus nature, too, speaks of an *active*
> God, of God the Father's continual search for man. Every sun-
> beam is his messenger. But this view arose out of Jesus' conscious-
> ness of that work of the Father which had been revealed to him,
> and which he himself was called to perform.[34]

It is not difficult to see the difference between the prophets
of the Old Testament and Jesus with his entirely new work
that laid the foundation of the New Testament. In both cases
God operated along both an "external" and an "inward" line.
But the voice in the heart of the prophets drove them *out* into
the history of the *people*. There were events which were to be
interpreted. Jesus, on the other hand, did not interpret the
history of *one* people. For him the commission of the Father,
given in the Son's inner being and growing forth out of the

Son's compassionate disposition toward every individual—
this commission of the Father was the all-important matter.
The generosity expressed in sun and rain was just a comple-
ment, a confirmation. The decisive historical event took place
in his own inner being: "Now first he understood fully the
secret of his nature. . . . Now he knew his Father fully. Now
he knew also what his work was to be."[35]

God's new action is to go to every *individual* with healing
and forgiveness of sins. It is a work given exclusively to the
Son, an action that transcends the limits of the people and
includes all the afflicted individuals in the whole world. But
on the basis of this new course of the life of Jesus new external
events will also happen in history: the death on the cross, the
resurrection on the third day, the gospel's penetration of the
Empire. This whole sequence was a new, tremendous deliverance out of Egypt, a new exodus, which the apostles, especially
Paul, were commissioned to interpret, just as the prophets in
the Old Covenant had interpreted the Exodus of the people
of Israel.[36]

But we have anticipated the events. First Judaism must
appear, first the *law* must "come in" (Rom. 5:20).[37]

## 2. The People (Grace) and the Individual (Law)

In a certain sense Billing's theology transcended the typical
Lutheran contrast between law and gospel, *jenseits von Gesetz
und Evangelium*. The doctrine of creation, as we have seen,
filled no independent role. Exodus absorbed Genesis. Since
creation and the law belong together, the law, too, played no
independent role in God's dealings with humanity. Billing
seems to mean that classical prophetism in Israel, and later in
Jesus himself, represented what in Lutheran dogmatics used
to be called "the original state," or "Paradise." God's commandments appeared then directly out of God's merciful acts.
The commandment was there already and functioned without

codification and without a book, but it did not impose an intolerable burden on man and did not condemn him to destruction. This was Billing's picture of the healthy prophetism where history was alive as the bearer of the new acts of God. When the law "came in," it caused a *derailment*. Then history was emptied of actions, and also of God's mercy. This was the travail of Judaism. The fortunes of the people appeared as "a dark water."[38] Only God's stern demands in the law were left.

We are not going to devote too much space to this development that Billing regarded as a deviation. But Judaism is so significant as a background of Jesus' proclamation that in the present context an account of its legalistic religion is necessary. Billing's conception of Judaism becomes most clear if we concentrate our attention at three points: Deuteronomy, Ezekiel, and 2 Esdras.* He subjected these three books to a thorough analysis.

His exposition of King Josiah's reformation and of Deuteronomy depended, of course, on the exegetical research at the turn of the century, but his fundamental point of view is well balanced and has historical value even today. According to Billing, Deuteronomy was the clearest line of demarcation in the whole of Israel's spiritual history. It summarized everything that had gone before and staked out the path of what was to come later. Deuteronomy wanted to secure for the ideas of the *prophets* the most eminent place in Israel. In a certain sense it succeeded in this effort, because the idea of *election* formed the fundamental basis for the book.[39] But at the same time it laid emphasis on two stations on the way through the wilderness: Mt. Horeb and the land of Moab (Deut. 5:2 f. and 29:1 f.). To these two Deuteronomy attached its second great idea, the *covenant*. There are, to be sure,

---

*Second Esdras, the "Ezra Apocalypse," is most commonly referred to in Swedish as 4 Esdras. (*Trans.*)

earlier traces of this concept of the covenant, but through the way in which Deuteronomy combined "election" and "covenant" a new synthesis appeared. This turned the attention away from God's unexpected acts in history to the system of justice that regulated the relationship between Yahweh and the people.[40] This system of justice did not really reckon with the possibility of any "surprises" on the part of God. The law "came in" and reduced the factors creating history to two: the obedience (or disobedience) of the people and God's retribution. Thus the law—not history—became the source for Israel's knowledge of God's will and his purposes.[41]

The concept of election is "condensed history, nothing else." The covenant idea did, to be sure, rest on God's act in history, on grace, but it lived in the law.

> If one assumes the point of view of the Deuteronomic concept of the covenant, one can obtain a bird's-eye view of the whole spiritual history of Judaism. In the original documents of Israel's ancient history one can see how the legal element grew at the expense of history, . . . how the superficial here found an excellent playground for their ingenuity, while the serious souls groaned under it as under an ever more oppressive yoke, . . . how the God of history himself receded from their view behind his substitute, the law.[42]

But Deuteronomy marked just the start in this direction. The storm wind of prophetism continued to roar through the legal paragraphs. But worse days would come. The connection between the individual and the events of history was to become ever more tenuous. It became Ezekiel's task to isolate the individual completely and render him *alone*. And "alone" meant alone with the *law*. Centuries were to pass before a liberator would come with the word of election and forgiveness to the individual.

Ezekiel was not only more "Jewish" than his contemporaries, but he surpassed even many who followed him in his emphasis on radical individualism. In the land of the Exile,

away from the national life in Palestine, the law gained
greater stature. According to Ezekiel, God no longer dwelt
down there among his people. After the fall of Jerusalem he
sat enthroned above the cherubim and *remained* there (Ezek.
10:18). "Now the law *alone* was left."[43] With unbelievable
boldness Ezekiel broke the bonds that had tied the individual
both to the forefathers and to the children, both to Israel's
past and to the future "unto the third and fourth generation."
The proverb about the fathers who had eaten sour grapes and
the children's teeth being set on edge was meaningful, as it
incorporated the individual into a long sequence of generations. But Ezekiel cut these bonds with one stroke: "As I live,
says the Lord God, this proverb shall no more be used by you
in Israel" (Ezek. 18:3). The individual stands absolutely alone
under the threatening retribution, with the law as a mirror
telling him what he is. In his own individual life he will reap
what he has sown, the evil as well as the good.[44]

Furthermore, the life of the individual "became severed into
two parts which were entirely separated." The line of division
was *conversion*.[45] If I "turn from wickedness," my earlier
sins will not be reckoned against me (Ezek. 33:11). If I fall
away, all my previous righteousness becomes worthless
(33:12 ff.). Conversion is an instrument in my hand. I can use
it of my own free will, and then it gives life; I can neglect it,
also of my own free will, and the result is death.

But how do life and death come to the individual? The
recompense comes in history, in the ordinary course of life.
This is the terrible residue of "the conception of history."
God gives evil and good in what happens from day to day.
Israel was tied to history and could not escape it. But now
history was on the way to becoming that curse under which
Job cried out in anguish. That the righteous suffer and the
wicked prosper is an observation which can torment every
individual among all people. But Judaism dogmatized the

misfortunes of life by incorporating them into a relationship
of the individual to his God. It increased the burden of suffering a thousandfold and located the torment in *conscience*.[46]
One may surmise even in this context that to break this evil,
dogmatized chain will require that one absolutely innocent
person be put to death among the wicked. He will then pre-
pare the way for an entirely new act of God in history and
will provide an "exodus" for every tortured individual soul
with a word of forgiveness.

As a result of the individualizing process, Ezekiel became
a *pastoral counselor*, "the first great counselor in Israel."[47] The
old prophets had spoken to whole nations and cities; Ezekiel
sought the individual with warnings and consolation—as much
consolation as he could give. He could individualize the law,
and he could individualize retribution and assign it to the
daily successes or misfortunes of every man. But when he
came to the consolation, he stood at an impassable frontier.
He could not individualize election. He could not grant the
individual an "exodus out of Egypt." He could not go to one
who was alone and say: "Your sins are forgiven."[48] No Old
Testament prophet dared to assume this extreme authority and
power; it would have meant that the prophet had made himself God. That the Jewish people had learned the location of
the impassable frontier was finally seen quite clearly when
there came one who possessed more than the authority of a
prophet and who said to a lame man not only, "Take up your
bed and walk"—many could have said that with power—but
what is more, "My son, your sins are forgiven" (Mark 2:5).
On that day the scribes were not shocked by the healing. It
was the forgiveness of sins that disturbed them. "Why does
this man speak thus? It is blasphemy! Who can forgive sins
but God alone?" (Mark 2:7). This New Testament passage
in all its brevity reveals more of the inner destitution of
Judaism than many long rabbinical texts.

Ezekiel was a pastoral counselor without access to a word of absolution. This was also true of Israel as a whole.[49] *Grace* lay embedded in those acts which God had done for the *people*. The divine election applied only to the people. The individual had no history of election which applied to him as such. The *individual* had received the *law*. He could examine himself with the help of the commandments and arrive at an estimation differing from that arrived at by his neighbor. In the area of morality, the Jewish people were separated into thousands of lonely individuals who examined themselves in the mirror of the law. There was no limit, on this level, to the individualizing process. But when every lonely soul looked up to God and his acts of mercy, it was the great "deliverances" which were the miracle of grace: out of Egypt and out of Babylon. These were the evidences of the Lord's mercy toward his *people*. The longer the road that Judaism traveled, the further grace receded into the past.[50] *The lone individual had received no exodus for himself*. The individual remained in the Egypt of the law, and he could not march out. It would have been a revolt against God if he had tried. And if anyone were to come with authority and *lead* him out with a word of forgiveness, then this savior would be a blasphemer. Such a Moses would not be able to avoid the cross.

If one cannot march out, one has to be satisfied with seeking mitigation. Judaism's balancing of righteousness and mercy was an attempt to find leniency in a house where "the chastisement of the Lord" took place. The older prophets could hold righteousness and mercy together in unity because God's act of election, his act of justice in history, the mercy that secured justice for the oppressed, was near to them.[51] God's mercy in history was near at hand, not far away, and mercy *itself* was righteousness. It was an act of justice which raised up the oppressed—an act such as no one is able to perform unless he is driven by love for the weak. Such an ethical stance is "condensed history." It can live only where the fresh winds of history blow, and where the events bear witness to the faithfulness of God. This ethical stance suffocates in the thin and stingy air of legalism, where one is compelled to balance one against another: severity as a general rule, indulgence at times; righteousness as the fundamental pattern, mercy as mitigation.

But if righteousness stands opposed to mercy, then neither one can be grace in the sense of *undeserved election.*[52] The Jewish point of view excluded the concept of grace; or, more precisely stated, this pure grace belonged exclusively to Israel's wonderful beginning, to the days of the Exodus. It was therefore excluded from the present and locked up in the past. Hope could wait for a similar miracle sometime in the future, but for the present one had to seek consolation in the thought that the trials were a *chastisement* by the Lord.

> Against the background of the extreme accentuation of this problem we must consider the last attempt of Judaism to escape from this terrible dilemma. It appears really in different variations, but they may be summarized in *one* formula: the sufferings of Israel and the righteous are "the chastisement of the Lord." Even if externally they appear as punishment, yes, even if they are that from one point of view, nevertheless in their inner meaning and purpose they are an expression of the Lord's thoughts of mercy directed toward his friends. He disciplines them in time in order to avoid judging them with the others.[53]

The Lord has not rejected the one whom he chastises. The heavenly Jerusalem of the future awaits those who are now suffering. But Billing thought that this apocalyptic conception was just an idea, and a rather barren one at that: "too thin an ice cover to quiet a sea in storm."[54] When Job and 2 Esdras spoke their own passionate language of the heart, they prayed, they insisted that God must intervene *now*—now, *at once!* They could not adjust to the endless delay.

Here we have already mentioned 2 Esdras, which Billing
regarded as after Deutero-Isaiah the greatest of Israel's
books.[55] Second Esdras carried the concept of retribution to
its ultimate, radical conclusion without balancing. God's punishment ends up in judgment. This is the radical element.
"And what good is it that an everlasting hope has been prom-
ised us, but we have miserably failed?"[56] Second Esdras'
prayer could therefore be a request for pure *grace*. When like
Job he cried to God and begged for a miracle in the present,
he prayed for divine mercy. And he presupposed that the
righteous God can have mercy upon the sinner, upon "those
who have no treasury of good works."[57] Although this thought
occurs only in a prayer, it represents the old classical unity of
righteousness and mercy, which we met in the oldest prophets
and in Deutero-Isaiah. But this unity could appear only in the
form of a prayer, because 2 Esdras knew of no *event* in history,
or, as Billing says, "no *fact* to which the idea of grace could
be attached."[58] Second Esdras is Paul *without* the event on
the Damascus road. He is without a *fact* to which he could
cling, constrained to resort to despair and prayer.

Even in a chronological sense the parallel to Paul is justi-
fied. Second Esdras belonged to Judaism, but he lived after
the conquest of Jerusalem by Titus. One generation had
passed since Jesus had finished his work. The gospel was
already on the way into Europe due to the work of Paul and
his successors. But nothing of this had affected 2 Esdras as
an *event*. He had been jolted by another "fact," the fall and
destruction of Jerusalem in A.D. 70.

> Even his thinking, like the thinking of the prophets, had its real
> center not in a supreme concept but in an epochal, historical
> event, an act of God in history, which he interpreted in his own
> way. This act was the conquest and destruction of Jerusalem. . . .
> This was the fact which had compelled him.[59]

Here we touch upon a principal point in Billing's biblical theology. To hold together righteousness and mercy, or judgment and grace, *is not a human possibility* unless history contains *events* in which God, the righteous and merciful One, *appears dealing with men in the present.*[60]

When Deutero-Isaiah could again "unite" his thoughts in the unique way of the classical prophets, he received, one could say, this unity as a gift through the course of events in which he lived: the exile to Babylon and the return from Babylon.

> Nowhere do the intimate unity of prophecy and history appear as clearly as here. Nowhere does one see so clearly that the prophet's view is not an elaborately developed system of heterogeneous thoughts. All that is necessary is that one of these tremendous acts of mercy establish anew the certainty of his presence, a certainty independent of thought and free from reflections. Then the thoughts are tied together again and *cannot* appear in any other form. And again, when this certainty is gone, no efforts of thinking are able to maintain this unity intact.[61]

Second Esdras lacked such an "act of mercy." In his prayers the idea of grace was pure, but it was removed from the earth, "unattainable by men," because "the act of election in the world" had not taken place.[62] One could not design grace.

Billing's exegetical method was critical, separating sources, dismembering. It is therefore very strange that he was able to mediate the impression of *unity* in the Bible more than any other writer I know of. It is just that unity which is suggested in so many Old Testament texts—Israel's unity. In Billing's analysis the people of Israel became *a person*. As a child Israel stood on the shores of the Red Sea praising God, and as a grown man he lived daily in this event. In his manhood the eroding reflection set in, forced by Deuteronomy. Then, after a short spring with Deutero-Isaiah on the way home

from Babylon, the long, despairing old age came. In his old
age he could do no more than appeal to God for pity. But
nothing happened. When we read Billing's analysis of 2
Esdras, we get the impression that this Jew *is* Paul, although
he has never stumbled upon the way where an act of election
takes place.

The unity of the Bible is real in Billing's thought, but
typically enough he discovered it through the means of
biblical criticism. As he worked objectively with the separation
and identification of sources, often expressing his gratitude to
Wellhausen, the unity of the Bible became even more evident
to him. This was really a remarkable combination.

### 3. Jesus and the Individual

When Billing proceeds to the New Testament documents,
we encounter the same unexpected combination, or twofold
stance. A great deal of his material is a biographical presentation of Jesus in the psychologizing style prevalent at the turn
of the century. But the reader nevertheless receives an impression of *unity*—in this case a unity between the life of
Jesus and the whole preceding development, all the way back
to the days of the Red Sea. When one reads Billing's description of Jesus' development, from his dependence on John
the Baptist to the clear conception of his own ministry, one
comes to an almost inevitable conclusion: Jesus of Nazareth
is truly *Ebed Yahweh*! In his struggle with the historical situation in which he was placed, he *became* the Suffering Servant.

John the Baptist proclaimed judgment. It is very probable
that the young Jesus belonged to his group.[63] The figures
which the Baptizer used reappeared in a new form in the
proclamation of Jesus, who revised them and made them
bearers of a new message.

There is first the tree and the axe. "Even now the axe is laid to the root of the trees; every tree therefore that does not bear good fruit is cut down and thrown into the fire" (Matt. 3:10). In John's preaching the tree without fruit is threatened with death. The only possibility of escape lies in repentance, in the production of good fruit. "The mightier" who is to come, and for whom John waits, has the tool in his hand and is ready to begin the work of judgment as soon as he arrives (Matt. 3:12). There is nothing else in the picture but judgment and the demand for repentance.[64] The fruits of repentance are the usual social duties of old: to share one's clothing and food with the poor, renounce violence against the weak, etc. (Luke 3:9–14). All this is in line with the good, prophetic pattern.[65]

When Jesus repeats the figure of the axe and the tree, he does not relax the element of judgment. The threat remains. "A man had a fig tree planted in his vineyard; and he came seeking fruit on it and found none" (Luke 13:6). The cutting down of the tree does not become a problem for discussion. If no fruit appears, the axe will go to work (see Luke 13:9). But what is new is a delay of execution, and what is really new is *a vinedresser who prays for grace* on behalf of the barren tree (Luke 13:8). In addition the expectation of "a mightier" is absent. The vinedresser who thus far has just been seeking a merciful way of escape for an Israel threatened with death *is* "the mightier" who was to come. But he does a work different from that predicted by the Baptizer. He does not wield the axe.[66]

The other set of figures speaks not of the axe and the tree, but of the wheat harvest, the chaff, the winnowing fork, and the threshing floor—and then again of the fire, the sign of judgment. "The mightier" whom John expects has the winnowing fork in his hand, "and he will clear his threshing floor

and gather his wheat into the granary, but the chaff he will
burn with unquenchable fire" (Matt. 3:12). In Jesus' proclamation this set of figures is transformed in a way that makes
them parallel to the vinedresser and his intercession. The fire
will burn, there is no question about that (Matt. 13:30), but
in regard to the work *in the present* the householder rejects
the servants' suggestion of an immediate removal of the weeds
in the same way as the praying vinedresser seeks to postpone
the cutting down of the tree. The servants' suggestion of a quick
weeding in the immediate present involves a *risk,* a risk threatening the *individual.* "No; lest in gathering the weeds you root
up the wheat along with them. Let both grow together until
the harvest" (Matt. 13:29 f.). The concern for the individual
stalk, which can only with difficulty be distinguished from the
weeds, determines what has to be done *now* in the present.
This concern is something totally new in comparison with
John the Baptist and his proclamation of judgment.[67]

To reckon with the imminent coming of the kingdom of
God, and yet to tarry with every individual: the paralytic, the
blind, the doubter—as Jesus did, according to the Gospels—
this was unique in Jesus' activity, and this procedure we find
in *none* of the Old Testament prophets. In this area a new
certainty must have come to Jesus himself, something which
he could not have found in any older writing or tradition. It
must have grown up in Jesus' own consciousness as he sought
to find his way. It was a search in two directions: upward to
the Father who will give the Son the *task* which he is to
perform *on behalf of the Father,* and outward to men who
suffer and who, most of all, are *in need of a shepherd.* Jesus
could not avoid having compassion for them, "harassed and
helpless" as they were, "like sheep without a shepherd" (Matt.
9:36). When these two concerns—the Father's command from
above and his own heart's immediate solidarity and sympathy

with the helpless—coalesced, then his certainty was established. His own emerging thoughts of mercy toward every
individual were the Father's thoughts of mercy toward man-
kind. But if they were the Father's thoughts, they could not
possibly remain mere "thought." Then *a task was given him,*
an entirely new act of election directed toward the individual.[68]
The *individual* was now to be brought out of the house of
bondage, out of Egypt.

In this way Billing always interpreted "the great word,"
"the great pronouncement about himself," "the great word of
jubilee" (Matt. 11:25–30; Luke 10:21–24).[69] "All things . . .
rest for your souls." When Jesus knew the Father, he turned
to the heavy laden with an invitation. Then his knowledge of
God became a work with people, a work which the Father
"had delivered" to the Son, or, in other words, which he had
entrusted to Jesus to perform on earth.

> And now we must note how Jesus' words, after he has made the
> most exalted statement that could be made about his communion
> with God, immediately issue not in a statement but in an act, in
> this invitation to all who labor and are heavy laden: Come to
> me. . . . Like the prophets before him, Jesus had received a com-
> mission from God. He had a work of God to perform, but for
> this task he had an unlimited authority such as no prophet had
> ever received. He had the authority to act in every respect on
> behalf of the Father. . . .[70]

This "all things" that had been delivered to him was *the work
of the Father,* and this in turn was carried out when he came
to the heavy laden with "rest for your souls" (Matt. 11:29).
"Now for the first time he understood the secret of his own
being. . . . Now he knew the Father fully. Now he knew also
what his work would be."[71]

Into this context Billing incorporated Jesus' constant practice of declaring forgiveness of sins to *individuals*—a practice

well documented in the whole gospel tradition. Such conduct
was unknown in the Old Testament. No prophet had acted in
that way. The narrative about the paralytic (Mark 2:3–12;
Matt. 9:2–8; Luke 5:17–26) shows that the scribes noticed
this new element and regarded it as blasphemy. If one forgives
the sins of an individual, one places oneself on the level of
God and *does God's work*. In his answer to the criticism of
the scribes Jesus affirmed that the specific authority *given* to
him (Matt. 9:8) was his "authority on earth to forgive sins"
(Mark 2:10; Matt. 9:6; Luke 5:24). He also affirmed that his
healing of the sick served in the interest of *this* authority, the
highest divine prerogative he had received from the Father.[72]
The conflict between Jesus and his surroundings which appears here caused three seemingly quite different elements to
become *one* in Jesus' consciousness: his certainty about the
nature of the Father; his responsibility for abused humanity,
"the sheep without a shepherd"; and his premonition that the
end might be the cross if he did not give in to the pressure of
his surroundings. The quiet work with individuals, one person
at a time, grew toward something much greater—death. Even
beforehand he reckoned with death as a consequence of his
fulfillment of the work received from the Father.[73]

In this context, both the continuity and the discontinuity
of Jesus' work with the old Israel and Judaism are of positive
importance. Jesus' Father is Israel's God and Father, he who
gave Israel its exodus from Egypt. Now he offers a new
exodus out of the house of bondage; not to a people this time,
but to every heavy laden individual whom Jesus meets. But
the new house of bondage was a prison for *individuals* that
had come into being through Israel's loss of the buoyant
thought of election and through its inability to interpret its
later history. The law had enslaved the life of the individuals
and had rendered them alone in judgment. No prophet could
point to an act of election for individuals.

> As soon as the prophet entered a little further into this develop-
> ment, the connection was broken with that from which his procla-
> mation derived all its singular features, certainty, and strength:
> the history interpreted in a religious sense, the history of election.
> . . . Jesus could give to the individual an ethical guidance of the
> same nature as the prophet had given to his people, because he
> could give to every one his own history of election, a history that
> was already beginning.[74]

Forgiveness of sins, given through Jesus' encounter with each individual, was the exodus offered to the lonely, his "exit out of Egypt."[75]

But Billing did not forget the element of judgment in Jesus' ministry. In his transformation of John the Baptist's two symbols of quick cleansing, the axe and the winnowing fork, Jesus, as we remember, did not let the idea of judgment disappear. Fire, the symbol of judgment par excellence, remained explicit even after Jesus' transformation of the pictures. There are in Jesus' proclamation a number of typical words of judgment directed to the contemporary world. Even in respect to the objects of his judgments, Jesus appeared as a classical prophet. He did not, in the first place, criticize the low morality of the masses; rather, the opposite. Again and again in new variations he denounced the *leaders* of the people, the learned scribes, those officials who corresponded to "the judges in the gate" of the old Israel. When Jesus "had compassion" for the multitudes, "the sheep without a shepherd," his spontaneous mercy contained at the same time an element of judgment. The other side of mercy was "his fierce anger against those who were guilty of this neglect," those who "bind heavy burdens, hard to bear, and lay them on men's shoulders" (Matt. 23:4; Luke 11:46).[76] This was in the ancient Israelite tradition of the true prophet. The merciful one secured justice for the oppressed.[77] Deutero-Isaiah's "grace and righteousness" reappeared in Jesus' proclamation (cf. Luke 18:7).[78]

The election of the individual, an election identical with the *forgiveness of sins,* the new exodus out of Egypt, stands in the Gospels in direct connection with Jesus' severe judgment on the leaders of the people. They were the ones who regarded this new exodus for the oppressed as blasphemy against God (cf. the narrative of the healing of the paralytic). " 'This man receives sinners and eats with them' (Luke 15:2). This was the most serious accusation the leaders of the people could make against him, and this accusation finally condemned him to death."[79] Justice and mercy, grace and righteousness, held together in this radically new election of *individuals,* unique in Israel's history, drove Jesus forward on his lonely way to death.

> But if the choice had to be made, if he had to be either judge or shepherd and protector of *individuals,* then he had to be fully and completely one with these individuals. He had to be really one of them, so that he could come near to even the lowliest among them, as brother to brother, as the shepherd to the lamb. He had to be prepared to accept all the bitterness of misunderstanding and enmity that such a ministry carried out in this way would entail. In this sense the way of Jesus was prescribed. He stood in conflict with all messianic expectations. His manner frequently caused offense even among those who relatively best understood him. But he himself could not hesitate.[80]

Unquestionably, the way was difficult. He was *tempted.*[81] But he went to the cross, a destiny made necessary by the combination of righteousness and mercy.

But righteousness and mercy were not only combined in such a way that the judgment on the scribes raised the lowly out of the dust, according to the old prophetic pattern. There was another much deeper combination, sensed even in the conscience of the lowly and arising directly out of the reception of forgiveness. The strikingly simple parable of the unmerciful servant (Matt. 18:23–35) whose lord forgave him a debt of ten thousand talents and who later demanded that his poor fellow servant pay him the paltry sum of a hundred denarii, reveals an ethical demand implicit in the word of forgiveness.[82] At one point the Lord's Prayer also provides an opportunity for ethical self-examination in connection with *the forgiveness of sins.*

> At the point in the Lord's Prayer where the most exalted work of the Father appears, the ethical demand makes itself known most insistently; so much so that the prayer is interrupted for a moment. One cannot pray "forgive us our trespasses" if one cannot say "as we forgive. . . ." It is clear that Jesus' thought of God as Father *included* all the other thoughts: holiness, righteousness, his power to punish—without limit. But in a way unheard of in Judaism he dared to make everything these terms contained the *means* for carrying out the Father's thoughts of mercy. God's almighty power . . . serves *entirely* his mercy.[83]

In *The Atonement (Försoningen)* Billing discussed at length that apocalyptic expectation of a coming judgment on Israel which must have characterized the followers of John the Baptist. He described Jesus' inner struggle as a liberation from John's pattern of judgment, although Jesus himself also maintained that judgment was inevitable. After a long struggle Jesus became convinced that the work given him by the Father to accomplish *now* was the forgiveness of sins. But a day would come when the axe would cut, the chaff would be blown away, and the fire would burn (Luke 13:9 and Matt. 13:30).[84] This tension between an immediate, scandalously quiet service toward individuals through forgiveness and healing (to which John reacted negatively, Matt. 11:2 ff.), on the one hand, and an approaching violent judgment, on the other, Billing incorporated into his great synthesis of righteousness and mercy, grace and justice. In part this was simply a temporal sequence: forgiveness now, judgment later. But on the basis of many traditional words of Jesus, words which undoubtedly are original and authentic, Billing was convinced that Jesus regarded himself as *empowered to judge now* (cf.,

for example, Matt. 26:53; Luke 9:54 f.; the struggle against
Satan according to Matt. 12:25–32; the confession before the
Sanhedrin, Mark 14:62).[85] The accounts of Jesus' "temptations," which likewise must belong to the oldest strata in the
gospel tradition, become meaningful only if Jesus himself was
certain of possessing an *authority* which could be used for
something other than the ministry of service which he had
chosen, or which *had been given* to him. But in his inner
struggle he rejected again and again this other use of his
power and remained "obedient." Billing included all this in
his synthesis of judgment and grace, righteousness and mercy.

But it is obvious that no synthesis can be established if one
component simply follows the other in a purely temporal
sequence. According to Jesus' thought, forgiveness occurs
now, judgment will come afterwards. (In the original version
this judgment may not have been conceived of in such universal terms as it later came to have in the apocalyptic pattern.
In the beginning most of it concerned only Israel.)[86] What
made a synthesis possible, however, was the fact that *the course
of events* inevitably moved forward *to the death on the cross.*
Although the course that Jesus chose (or "was given"), the act
of forgiveness which demolished the power of the law over the
individual, was regarded as sacred by many, it was of such a
nature that it could end in nothing but the crucifixion, with its
unity of judgment and grace. His death, therefore, was not "a
suffering of punishment" in the sense of the doctrine of satisfaction. But it *was vicarious.* The death on Golgotha was a
death which Jesus suffered on behalf of many individuals.
This understanding even characterized Jesus' own interpretation before the death occurred.[87] He could at any time have
avoided the cross if he had been willing to desist from his
scandalous practice, if he had been willing to betray the word
of forgiveness which was the individual's exodus out of the
house of bondage. Because he would not cease from bestowing

exodus out of Egypt, he became the Suffering Servant and died on Golgotha. History, the inevitable march of events, brought forth something *new*.

> What drove him into death was the opposition to that grace which is available even to the sinner and to that righteousness which judges even the righteous. He saw this opposition to him as a sign that this generation's own unrighteousness rendered it ripe for judgment (Matt. 23:35 f.). His love was strong enough to endure death for these wicked ones and once again to pray for them. But to buy relief by making concessions to unrighteousness was impossible for him. Not only God's love, which breaks through all the rules of righteousness, became victorious in Jesus' death, but also that righteousness which firmly maintains its opposition to all unrighteousness.[88]

When we read Billing's rather psychologizing exposition of how Jesus was tempted and yet was able to persist in his course, we have a definite feeling that the unity of righteousness and mercy which ancient Israel once found in an historical event, the exodus out of Egypt and the deliverance at the Red Sea, and which the same Israel kept ethically intact in its care for the lowly, was in danger of being lost. The unity could not be regained in the people as a people. The destruction of Jerusalem and the despair of 2 Esdras already loomed on the horizon. Only in one single person did righteousness and mercy dwell in unity without thought of retribution and without lax indulgence. This lone one had already outgrown the limited historical situation of the chosen people. The exodus he bestowed applied to individuals, but this meant it applied to *all*. It was available to every single individual, no matter to what people he belonged. This lonely one had invisible resources which were to become available to all humanity.[89]

The power residing in him was the power of "the grain of wheat," to use his own language. Ultimately only one task remained to be done: "to fall into the earth and die."

## 4. Death and Resurrection

Two aspects of Billing's interpretation of Jesus' death and resurrection are especially noteworthy. In the first place, the death stands in the context of Jesus' total mission; it results from his own inner consciousness and from his purely historical ministry on earth. It is just in this sense that his death became *vicarious*. Billing did not operate with an isolated, *atoning* death, conceived of as a suffering of punishment, with God as the recipient of the sacrifice.[90] In the second place, Billing incorporated the *resurrection* into Jesus' total ministry and viewed it as a continuation of *the ministry of forgiveness* extended to *all people*. Billing was not interested in the resurrection as a miracle intended to "validate" the effect on God of the atoning death.[91] In his thought, the resurrection of Christ became ("somewhat one-sidedly" as Billing says in gentle self-criticism) the living presence of Christ with his own. "I am with you always, to the close of the age" (Matt. 28:20).[92]

Both of these elements in Billing's thought, his interpretations of Jesus' death and of his resurrection, had parallels in contemporary and later theology, especially in Germany. In regard to Jesus' inner consciousness we could note Wilhelm Herrmann, whom Billing himself mentioned. We could also think of Martin Kähler, as acknowledged by Billing, in connection with the resurrection and its rapid identification with the continuing preaching of the gospel. Among the moderns we could mention Bultmann.[93] But the parallels apply in these cases to single aspects, while the whole structure is something unique to Einar Billing. Furthermore, his whole work is characterized by an unusually systematic coherence.[94]

It is best to begin with the interpretation of Jesus' death and its vicariousness as inherent in "the historical Jesus" and his ministry. Billing contended that our time is different from *all* past times in that *the person* of Jesus Christ, and nothing else, must constitute the only possible "foundation of faith" in any discussion of an "atonement."

> If we mean by the "foundation" of faith that in which our faith in the living God first finds anchorage against *doubts* and that to which, when doubts again emerge and threaten to make everything insecure, faith can again return as to a secure rock, then we cannot seek this "foundation of faith" in Jesus' "atoning death." It must be sought elsewhere. Where? Without hesitation or reservation I join with those who answer this question by pointing to the person of Jesus Christ, "the historical Christ." I can gladly add that here I think especially of the form this answer has received in Wilhelm Herrmann's writings. This term, "the historical Christ," has undeniably often served as a slogan for a certain theological tendency, and has therefore become suspect to others, not only those on the right but also those on the left. . . . This is unfortunate. I believe that *everyone* would otherwise easily perceive that this answer comes from his own inner consciousness. It points to a *fundamental* peculiarity in the situation of Christian faith in our time. This situation is common not only to certain groups but to us all, and is therefore worthy of contemplation by all in the interest of the clarity and certainty of faith. Our time questions much of what our forefathers accepted as immediate and unshakable certainty, and which at least *appeared* to them as the real foundation of faith—although in the last analysis that foundation is always the same. Among these certainties we can mention as examples the inspired book, the old christological dogmas, etc. In reality this questioning affects us all, although not everybody has become fully conscious of this fact. But the person of Jesus Christ as pictured in the Gospels has lost nothing of its old power to overwhelm and subjugate a man as he proceeds through life. Christ is like a cliff which man cannot pass by, a *reality* which man recognizes and cannot deny. If man will not say anything else about this reality, he must at least admit his difficulty in incorporating it into such reality as he otherwise admits knowing. Yes, one could even say that the person of Christ has won an additional reservoir of strength, has *increased* in immediate power of persuasion, at least in part because these same factors have eroded those elements that were earlier accepted as foundations of faith.[95]

These words, first spoken in 1907 and published in print in 1908, were for a long time outdated, but now have again become quite modern. After the dizzy victory of kerygmatic

theology and the consequent depreciation of "the historical
Jesus," we are back approximately to the position which
Billing held after the turn of the century. But Billing's perspective backward to Israel's deliverance from Egypt and
forward to the normal, ongoing, quite unpretentious ministra-
tion of the means of grace in the church was not usually an
element in the discussion at the turn of the century, nor does
it play any essential part in the present renaissance. Billing
carried on an unusually incisive analysis of the concepts of
election and the covenant in the Old Testament, the latter
arising out of the same idea of election but following a separate development through Ezekiel and Judaism down to 2
Esdras. On the basis of this analysis Billing understood Jesus'
earthly ministry from its purely *Jewish* presuppositions. In one
sense, therefore, "the historical Christ" became localized in a
specific situation both geographically (only in Israel) and tem-
porally (in the era of apocalyptic). It might seem, therefore,
that Jesus could not be of any significance for other people
after he had, in Billing's analysis, been so definitely identified
with a specific milieu. But the result was the very opposite.
When all the threads in the description of the milieu were
drawn together into a single point, Jesus' ministry appeared
as a total *disintegration* of that particular milieu, Judaism, and
at the same time as the most profound fulfillment of the
*mission* of this limited milieu *to other nations*. When the
milieu was shattered, exodus, exit, liberation became available
to every individual person. Israel then came to be in the
world what its election originally had intended it to be, "a
light to the nations" (Isa. 42:6 and 49:6).[96]

This single point to which all the threads in the description
of the milieu led was the word of the forgiveness of sins
addressed to individuals in the context of Jewish legal piety.
This word—"your sins are forgiven"—was in this situation so
loaded with explosive power that the whole structure of the

law fell and the final eschatological miracle occurred: God himself came and spoke through the mouth of a man. But at the same time this word was not miraculous from the point of view of natural science. There is nothing whatever unbelievable in this word, even for a critical historian. On the contrary, we follow Billing's psychological description of the suffering that the idea of retribution caused among sensitive Jews, and of Jesus' own "thoughts of mercy" as he went about among the people and saw the "sheep without a shepherd"; but nowhere in this psychological reasoning do we find any suggestion of *myth*. Furthermore, that such a merciful person projected his own thoughts of mercy onto the Father in heaven and thereby received "a divine mission among men," that, too, appears entirely and historically authentic. There is no myth here either.[97] That this mission of dispensing the forgiveness of sins aroused the *anger* of the leaders of the people, and that this mission led him to the *cross*—this, too, is something which can be understood only on the basis of the specific Jewish milieu. According to Billing, that milieu was a derailment, a deviation from Israel's fundamental course.[98]

A "demythologizing" program appeared, therefore, in Billing's theology as early as 1907, but without some of the features which later characterized demythologizing in Europe. The messianic claim was acknowledged, although it was hidden under "the work of the Father" and under "the power to forgive sins." Last, but not least, no philosophy of existentialism was utilized in the interpretation of the human situation. That Jesus' death was a vicarious death "for the many" is fully understandable from the nature of the act of forgiveness. He could save his life only by betraying the many. If he was faithful to the many (i.e., if he continued his scandalous practice of forgiveness), he would have to pay for his faithfulness by death on the cross. Even when the death at Golgotha entered the picture, no myth was brought in. His death was incorporated into his life's mission as a necessary consequence of the ministry carried on by "the historical Jesus." His death was objectively a death for the many precisely in the sense in which an ordinary historian views a plausible happening. It was just as objective as a situation in which a man remains at his post in a war and thereby dies on behalf of the inhabitants of a city. Not even at this final point, when Jesus died as the *vicarious representative,* do we find in Billing any trace of myth. Everything is history. We do not now need to interpret and transform the myth into history. Everything *is* history.[99]

And now—the perspective in the other direction, forward into the history of the church! It is a simple fact that the gospel of the forgiveness of sins was preached in the Mediterranean world shortly after Jesus' death, and that thus "the church" arose. According to Luther, all the means of grace mediate the forgiveness of sins, nothing else. Precisely from the point of view of the historical Christ does it become understandable that the church on earth has the appearance it has.

If we keep this starting point in mind and contemplate the progress of the gospel, "the word," through the world, it is as if we were seeing the Lord Christ himself wandering from country to country in order to fulfill his promise also to seek and to "draw to himself" the "other sheep," whom he had not reached during his ministry on earth. Only in this way would there be "one flock, one shepherd" (John 10:16). As means for the clarification of the Spirit's work in building the church and for our understanding of that structure, we have available nothing less than the Lord's total ministry here on earth. When he wandered from village to village and preached the gospel, the crowds came to him from near and far. Those who then listened to him represented the most varied spiritual conditions. Many of those who listened to his word never came near to him in their own hearts, and others who for a time seemed to belong to him finally took offense and went away. Just so it continues to be whenever the invisible Lord through the word and the Spirit goes about among men even today.[100]

In this quotation we recognize not only the church as it actually is, but also the *national* church as it really is with "the most varied spiritual conditions" represented. The whole picture is dominated by him who "goes about" among these people, offering to all his exodus, just as Jesus actually did on earth before his death.

In this context there is a strange inevitability in Billing's conception. Jesus went to his death *in order* to be able "to continue forgiving," and in order not to betray the ministry given him by the Father. Only by going to his death, says Billing, could Jesus "save his life as the forgiver of sins."[101] The resurrection on the third day has a similar inevitability related to it. Billing brushed aside all speculation concerning the resurrection as a validation of Christ's death as an efficacious suffering of the punishment for man's sin. Christ arose —again—*in order* "to continue forgiving." He breaks through the barriers, goes out to other suffering individuals among all nations of the world, and with his gospel opens the possibility of exodus for us all.[102] I do not believe that anyone else in Billing's generation spoke of the resurrection in this fashion. This picture was an original combination of "the historical Jesus" with "the forgiveness of sins," and thus formed a great, unifying concept. It included Jesus' ministry on earth in the region of Galilee, the death on the cross, the resurrection on the third day, and his presence through the means of grace in the church until the Parousia. What I myself have written about preaching and the gospel from 1949 until now has been strongly influenced by Billing's work, his influence having been far stronger than that of continental kerygmatic theology.[103]

We do not find anywhere in Billing's writings an isolated description of the resurrection on the third day as an event *in itself*. On this point Billing manifested an obvious reserve, which was not due exclusively to a scientist's hesitation to accept a miracle. The deeper reason was Billing's fear of the irresponsible and bombastic language employed in nearly all speech concerning an isolated miracle which occurred contrary to natural laws. This strained fervor of faith does not help the struggling man of today. There is just one thing he can cling to in the hour of doubt: the person of Christ, the human person of Christ, who in solidarity with us turns to each of us "as brother to brother, as the shepherd to the lamb." It is a solidarity which, in the face of approaching death on the cross, grows into a suffering and powerless solidarity with "the many."[104] Even before the crucifixion these "many" were, in Jesus' thought, an indefinite number. The sum total is a priori *open*. From one point of view the resurrection was the surprising discovery by the disciples that the number of the many is limitless, infinite. The number grows over the boundaries of peoples and tongues and down through the generations in time. The horizon opens in all directions wherever one looks. *This is the resurrection from the dead, a continuous exodus.*[105]

In his interpretation of the death and resurrection of Christ, Billing emphasized the synthesis between righteousness and mercy. He claimed that he could support this interpretation with the letters of Paul (Rom. 3:26, 3:31, 4:25, 5:12–21, 8:3, 8:32; 2 Cor. 5:18–21; Gal. 2:21, 3:13, 3:24; and several other passages).[106] In God himself righteousness and mercy were *one* when Jesus suffered and conquered. God acted both in judgment and in grace when Jesus carried through his ministry on earth. But earlier, when Billing dealt with such "acts of judgment by the living God" (the deliverance from Egypt, the return from Babylon, Jesus' unconditional forgiveness of the sinner), he immediately, as we have seen, pointed out the implications of these acts for *ethics*.[107] On this subject we do not find very much from the Pauline letters in Billing's books, and on this point he practically ignored the Pauline ethics.[108] This was obviously due to his choice of subject. He dealt with the Old Testament and the Gospels in *The Ethical Thoughts (De etiska tankarna),* and he discussed the Pauline letters in *The Atonement.*

If, on the contrary, we were to make ethics our theme in dealing with death and resurrection, we would immediately encounter the Pauline concept of "following" and "imitation." The Christian becomes conformed to Christ in death and resurrection. This is a realization of the meaning of *baptism,* and it is carried out in acts directed toward "the neighbor" and "the others," acts which are often quite commonplace. It is easy to see what excellent material such an ethic of baptism offers, especially if one wants to show how God's judgment and grace become *one* on the level of human activity, and how "the poor are lifted out of the dust" through these acts which originate in baptism. All these were common, almost shopworn elements in Billing's synthesis of righteousness and mercy, but an exhaustive and thorough analysis of this subject is not to be found in Billing's published works. We have to do it ourselves.[109] But if we do it ourselves it can be done without violation to Billing's structure; we find ourselves at least to some extent within that structure. We then simply draw some additional consequences from what Billing himself has already done, especially in regard to the Old Testament.[110]

Nevertheless, we then find ourselves within Billing's structure only to a certain extent. His passivity in regard to certain materials threatened at times to become more than passivity and rendered the structure rigid rather than open. In general it might be said that the very idea of election, or "prevenient grace," took over everything and tended to dissolve the *demand* inherent in election. Billing's doctrine of baptism was thus thoroughly a doctrine of infant baptism, with the point polemically directed toward the free churches which practiced adult baptism, or baptism with commitment. Billing more or less neglected the aspect of baptism as a death and resurrec-

tion; consequently he also neglected the ethical implications
of baptism for everyday living. Death and resurrection as
ethical concepts dominated Luther's doctrine of the call and
gave rise to the singular notion of "the cross" in the calling.
Billing observed this feature of Luther's teaching, but he himself avoided using it. Billing's doctrine of the calling became
therefore céntered in the concept of election. My personal
history in work and home becomes a miniature of Israel's
history, with exodus at the beginning.[111] On this point Billing
consciously and deliberately departed from Luther.[112]

All of these points have to do with *death and resurrection*.
But at every point Billing refused to draw any consequences
in the area of *ethics*. One result of this refusal was that Billing's
conception of the national church became characterized by a
strange silence in regard to responsibility and commitment.
This characterized Billing's whole polemical attitude toward
the free churches. He stated very clearly and sharply that in
infant baptism grace comes *before* all human decisions. But
that something comes *after* grace in regard to human social
life did not become correspondingly clear. What are so surprisingly lacking here in Billing's view are the ethical implications of God's merciful act of judgment upon his people.
But these ethical implications were the very features in Israel's
view of history which Billing had emphasized from Moses
down to the ministry of Jesus.

The explanation of this change in emphasis is very probably
his specific interpretation of Luther and his polemic against
the free churches. We will return to this subject in the following chapter on Luther. But first, within the framework of this
biblical chapter, we must summarize briefly what constitutes
the nature of the church. Billing maintained that its foundation derived from the Bible, not from the Reformation.[113]
What the Reformers did, according to Billing, was to redis-
cover and make use of an old biblical conception.

## 5. The Nature of the National Church

Billing's most well-known Easter sermon was, typically enough, a sermon on the Second Day of Easter. It was, moreover, in almost all its parts a commentary on his hymn, Number 380 in the *Swedish Psalmbook* of 1937. The sermon dealt not with the events at the empty tomb but with what happened at Emmaus and with the disciples' return.

> What happened to the Emmaus disciples has also happened to all. It is the history of Paul after Damascus, and the history of all the apostles. This is the background of the word in which the disciples summarized everything they had learned during their association with the risen Lord: "Go into all the world and make disciples of all nations . . . ; and lo, I am with you always, to the close of the age." The same element is the background of the word in our text: "They arose that same hour and returned." It is only against this background that we can understand the significance of this detail. But it is interesting to define this great context in connection with just this detail. That Jesus rose on the day of Easter, and that on the Second Day of Easter the disciples rose up and returned to Jerusalem are two items in the same history.[114]

Billing's point was that the texts in the New Testament which tell of the post-Easter Christ as the living One are at the same time texts about *sending*. The witnesses "rose up" and went out with the word, the word that created the church. In this context the shattering of the narrow Israelite framework has an essential significance. Until the death of Christ Israel was the frame of reference for the whole history of election. The other nations were outside, waiting. But the old national frame broke slowly apart, even during the time of the old Israel, through the development of *individualism*. As soon as the Deuteronomic idea of the "covenant" began to supersede the concept of election, and as soon as the individual Israelite could look at himself and his actions in the mirror of the *law,* the possibilities for the individual to stand alone in a self-examination of his morality became greater and greater.[115] Ezekiel raised ethical *individualism* to its highest point, and 2 Esdras had to bear the burden of anxiety caused by this emphasis. All of them laid burdens on the individual, but no one provided him with an exodus.[116] Grace became tied down to actions concerned with the *people*. These actions were great events far back in the past, which at that time provided deliverance for the people, but which *did not now secure forgiveness for the individual*. Jesus was the first one who dared to assume this unprecedented authority. He was the first who gave "an exodus out of Egypt" to the lowly individual through the word of forgiveness addressed specifically to him.[117] This activity brought him to death on the cross for the many. This unique redeemer rose from the dead, and *his forgiveness operates now* through all those whom he sends. "Go therefore and make disciples of all nations . . . ; and lo, I am with you always . . ." (Matt. 28:19 f.).

This review of Billing's perspective of Israel's history shows that the *first* word which broke the national framework and reached out to the nations waiting on the outside was *the word of forgiveness from the living Christ*. The fruit of the long biblical history was the gospel of the forgiveness of sins, a gospel which can be called "condensed history," in the exact meaning of that phrase. The essential nature of this gospel is such that it must always be on the move *out there among the peoples of the world*. He who preaches this gospel to the nations does not preach a part of the Bible, he confers the *whole* content of the Bible on everyone who believes. Everything that happened in Israel happened in order that such an exodus might be given to every individual.[118]

This gospel of the forgiveness of sins is the foundation of the national church.[119] Billing incorporated his discussion of Jesus' death and resurrection directly into his analysis of the conception of the church. The result was that he defined the organizational pattern of the national church as the form most suitable to the gospel.[120] Traces of this reasoning are found as early as his book *The Atonement.*

> We may point to the whole history before and after Jesus' death. Before Jesus' death and resurrection the history which now continues preeminently in the history of the Christian church was limited to one nation. Since that time it has drawn nation after nation into its orbit. It has often been delayed, but never interrupted. If in our day we can begin to speak seriously of a common world history, and not least of a common "history of religion," many factors have contributed to this development. But what is it that has led the way? Undoubtedly, *world* mission! The New Testament declares: the time of preparation is past; now the call goes out (Matt. 22:4), "Go therefore and make disciples of all nations" (Matt. 28:19).[121]

But in his later writings concerning the national church the direct line from the forgiveness of sins to the form of the national church became *the principal theme.* He returned to this thought with almost wearisome persistence. This direct line, says Billing, is the most typical feature of his conception of the church.

> What is characteristic of this conception is the consistency with which the line is drawn directly from the most intensely religious center: the forgiveness of sins, unmerited, prevenient grace, forward not to the church in the abstract and ideal sense but to this concrete and realistically obvious—and imperfect—national church. I could as well say the Swedish national church in our country at this present time.[122]

There is therefore an unusually close connection between Billing's biblical theology and his concept of history.[123]

If, on the other hand, we note the terms used to establish this connection between the gospel and the church, the influence of Luther becomes more obvious than the part played by the Bible. Luther constructed his theology programmatically in such a way that the formal, structural element became a doctrine of two different realms. One of these, called *ecclesia,* or "the spiritual government," is ruled entirely by "the gospel." The other realm is ruled by "the sword," or by "the law." The completely dominant factor in the development of Luther's conception of the church was the forgiveness of sins, or *remissio peccatorum*. It was of decisive significance, both positively and negatively, that Billing began his scholarly production in 1900 with a treatise on Luther, and specifically with a treatise on Luther's conception of the *state*. A certain tendency to isolate the gospel from the law was therefore present in Billing's thought from the beginning. It was there long before Billing dealt with Greece and Israel in 1907 and 1908.[124] We will discuss this specific contribution from the Reformation and the sixteenth century in our next chapter.

## NOTES TO CHAPTER III

1. Einar Billing, *De etiska tankarna i urkristendomen* (2nd ed. enlarged; Stockholm, 1936), p. 74.

2. *Ibid.* We find in prophetism a completely different picture of man's situation. *Ibid.*, p. 122.

3. *Ibid.*, pp. 77 f.

4. *Ibid.*, p. 83. Cf. pp. 185 f., concerning Deutero-Isaiah, and p. 27, concerning Socrates.

5. *Ibid.*, p. 85. Cf. p. 398, concerning Jesus.

6. *Ibid.*, p. 105. Cf. pp. 100 f.

7. *Ibid.*, p. 102; also, p. 104.

8. *Ibid.*, p. 213. The teaching about "the two measures" is the succinct expression indicating that the genuine, prophetic unity has been lost.

9. *Ibid.*, p. 130 (italics mine). Billing cites a number of other passages from Israelite laws as proofs for his thesis.

10. Cf. *ibid.*, p. 64; also Einar Billing, *Försoningen* (2nd ed.; Stockholm, 1921), pp. 11–20.

11. *De etiska tankarna,* pp. 83 f.

12. *Ibid.*, p. 101.

13. *Ibid.*, p. 126. "Individual ethics" may also mean something else. Cf. Einar Billing, *Luthers lära om staten* I (Uppsala, 1900), p. 107.

14. *Ibid.*, p. 128.

15. *Ibid.*, pp. 92 f.

16. This point recurs frequently in Billing's writings. See his *De etiska tankarna*, pp. 93, 183–86 (concerning Deutero-Isaiah), 260–64; also his *Försoningen*, pp. 11–12, 100 f. (on the part played by world mission); and his *Herdabrev till prästerskapet i Västerås stift* (2nd ed.; Stockholm, 1962), pp. 54 f.

17. *De etiska tankarna*, pp. 64, 75; *Försoningen*, pp. 9–11.

18. *De etiska tankarna*, pp. 79–83. Cf. Einar Billing, *Our Calling*, rev. trans. Conrad Bergendoff ("Facet Books – Social Ethics Series," 1; Philadelphia: Fortress Press, 1964), pp. 8–17. In Billing's interpretation the idea of the calling is a variant of his conception of history.

19. *De etiska tankarna*, pp. 152–54. Deuteronomy is the portal into Judaism, where the characteristic features of classical prophetism have become lost.

20. *Ibid.,* p. 106.

21. Cf. *ibid.,* p. 4, concerning Aristotle.

22. Cf. *ibid.,* pp. 92 f. In Amos this view of the surrounding peoples is strongly accentuated (see Amos 9:7), and in Deutero-Isaiah monotheism is fully developed; this means that Israel in its destruction and death can become "a light to the nations" (Isa. 49:6, 53:10–22). See *Försoningen*, pp. 25 f., 39–41; also *De etiska tankarna*, pp. 181–83.

23. *De etiska tankarna*, pp. 130 f. (italics mine). Cf. pp. 265 f.; and Einar Billing, *Den svenska folkkyrkan* (2nd ed.; Stockholm, 1963), pp. 31, 34, 57.

24. At times the agreement between Job and Genesis is verbal. See Job 33:6, 10:9; and Gen. 2:7. Cf. *De etiska tankarna*, pp. 271–74, where the depreciative attitude dominates. Nevertheless, cf. Billing's article in *Vår lösen* (1912), p. 308, where he deals with a different context.

25. This lacuna exercises a powerful effect in the development of the conception of the national church in Billing's work. He interprets the church but *not* human life as such. The difference between Billing and a man like Grundtvig in Denmark is very pronounced, and affects later church history in both Sweden and Denmark. The kind of isolation that now characterizes the Church in Sweden is not possible in Denmark.

26. See *Den svenska folkkyrkan*, pp. 142–46.

27. When the doctrine of creation usurps the place of the conception of history, Judaism becomes lord over the religious heritage of the prophets and the classical view is lost. History becomes silent. See *De etiska tankarna*, pp. 282–85.

28. *Ibid.,* pp. 94–99.

29. *Ibid.,* p. 96.

30. *Ibid.,* pp. 95 f. We are reminded that in the New Testament the appearances of Jesus as the risen Lord are consistently interpreted as acts of *sending*.

31. *Ibid.*, p. 358; also, pp. 359–64, 374–84, 395 (very clearly), 404–10 (very clearly and comprehensively). See also *Försoningen*, pp. 74 f., 81, 122 f.

32. *Försoningen*, p. 75. Jesus gives "an exodus out of Egypt" to every individual. Billing interprets Matt. 11:27 f. similarly.

33. *De etiska tankarna*, p. 381. Cf. *Försoningen*, pp. 108 f.

34. *De etiska tankarna*, pp. 380 f.

35. *Ibid.*, p. 395. More extensively on pp. 404–9. Billing goes to great length to provide a biography of "the inner life" of Jesus. Cf. his defense of Wilhelm Herrmann in *Försoningen*, pp. 104–10.

36. *Försoningen*, pp. 70–102, 130–35; also Einar Billing, *I katekesundervisningens tjänst* (2nd ed.; Stockholm, 1963), pp. 95–98; *Herdabrev*, pp. 54–60.

37. *De etiska tankarna*, p. 7; an allusion to Wellhausen's *Prolegomena*.

38. *Ibid.*, p. 194, a quotation from the Apocalypse of Baruch. The expression recurs frequently; *ibid.*, pp. 195, 197, 221.

39. *Ibid.*, p. 136; cf. p. 154.

40. *Ibid.*, pp. 141–53.

41. *Ibid.*, pp. 154–56. Here is a point where Einar Billing and Anders Nygren work with similar presuppositions. See Anders Nygren, *Agape and Eros*, rev. trans. Philip S. Watson (Philadelphia: Westminster Press, 1953), pp. 67–71, where Nygren develops the significance of Jewish legal piety. But Nygren and Billing differ in their interpretation of Jesus' proclamation. The reason for the difference is that Billing's point of departure is the Old Testament, which is not the case in Nygren's motif research.

42. *De etiska tankarna*, pp. 157 f. When the canon was formed, the term "law" covered the whole history of Israel's origin. Exodus was incorporated into the law.

43. *Ibid.*, p. 161; cf. p. 160.

44. *Ibid.*, p. 162; cf. p. 168.

45. *Ibid.*, p. 165; cf. p. 163.

46. Note especially Deut. 28, the terrifying chapter on "blessing" and "curse."

47. *De etiska tankarna*, p. 161.

48. *Ibid.*, p. 164.

49. It is therefore at *this* point that Jesus makes a new start. *Ibid.*, p. 352; cf. pp. 306, 314, 351.

50. *Ibid.*, pp. 154, 197–99, 219, 284.

51. *Ibid.*, pp. 102–5.

52. *Ibid.*, p. 213; cf. pp. 227–29. Billing's conception of the doctrine of "the two measures" is negative. The reason for this is that one component in the comparison, prophetism, maintains a unique unity of righteousness and mercy. From *this* point of view the balancing as such becomes weakness, no matter how the details appear.

53. *Ibid.*, p. 246; cf. the reference to 2 Macc. 6:12–17, *ibid.*, p. 248.

54. *Ibid.*, p. 250; cf. p. 252.

55. On the relationship between 2 Esdras and the Apocalypse of Baruch see *ibid.*, p. 216 n. 3.

56. *Ibid.*, p. 226, direct quotation from 2 Esdras 7.

57. *Ibid.*, pp. 217 f.; long quotations from 2 Esdras 8 and 9.

58. *Försoningen*, p. 47. Cf. again *De etiska tankarna*, pp. 226, 185 f.

59. *Försoningen*, p. 46; cf. *De etiska tankarna*, p. 245.

60. See the important passage on Paul and Luther in *Herdabrev*, pp. 58 f. Bridges must therefore be built from the Bible to the present. The parish church is such a bridge.

61. *De etiska tankarna*, pp. 185 f. Billing regards it as important that Deutero-Isaiah again utilizes terms from the Red Sea pericope; the Exodus is repeated. However, cf. "Trito-Isaiah," *ibid.*, pp. 186–88. History is again silent.

62. See *ibid.*, p. 226. On the contrary, Paul could join the thoughts together. In his case something had *happened*.

63. Cf. *ibid.*, pp. 354, 401–8; also *Försoningen*, pp. 87–91.

64. *De etiska tankarna*, pp. 354–58, 400.

65. *Ibid.*, p. 351.

66. Especially *ibid.*, pp. 399 f., 401–4, also 355–59.

67. *Ibid.*, pp. 358, 407 f.

68. Along this line see a number of passages in *De etiska tankarna*, e.g., pp. 352, 358, 376, 384–95, 398–409. The divergence from John the Baptist's picture of the future thus becomes a fact. What John objects to in Jesus' messianic work is the specific direction of concern toward the individual (see Matt. 11:2–6).

69. *De etiska tankarna*, pp. 358, 409 (cf. 404), 394. See also *Försoningen*, pp. 74 f., 81, 121 f.; *I katekesundervisningens tjänst*, pp. 6 f., 12; and finally *Herdabrev*, pp. 53 f.

70. *De etiska tankarna*, p. 376.

71. *Ibid.*, p. 395; cf. p. 409.

72. *Ibid.*, pp. 306–14.

73. This feature of the work of the Father, the approaching death, stands in the center of Billing's book, *Försoningen;* see, e.g., pp. 77 f., 91–98, *et passim.*

74. *De etiska tankarna*, p. 352.

75. *Försoningen*, p. 75; cf. p. 22.

76. See *De etiska tankarna*, pp. 408, 341, 387, 402; also *Försoningen*, p. 88.

77. *Ibid.*, p. 403; cf. pp. 104 f., where the unified, prophetic view is expressed: "righteousness *is* mercy."

78. *Ibid.*, p. 371; cf. the great exposition of Deutero-Isaiah, pp. 179–86; and *Försoningen*, pp. 80 f.

79. *Försoningen*, p. 78; cf. *De etiska tankarna*, pp. 346–53.

80. *Försoningen*, p. 91.

81. About the temptation, see, e.g., *Försoningen*, pp. 92–97.

82. *De etiska tankarna*, pp. 369 f.; see n. 1 for a comparison of Judaism and Jesus' proclamation.

83. *Ibid.*, p. 370. Billing follows the primary text of Matt. 6:12, "have forgiven."

84. *Ibid.*, pp. 356 f., and especially 401–8. Jesus' transformation of the figures does not destroy the general framework created by John the Baptist.

85. *De etiska tankarna*, pp. 357, 356, 403 f.; cf. *Försoningen*, pp. 83–86.

86. See *Försoningen*, p. 85. The anticipated act of judgment could have begun with something like the cleansing of the temple (*De etiska tankarna*, p. 404). This act contains an element of violence which is not present in the rest of the ministry: the whip of cords, the overturning of the tables of the money changers, etc.

87. See *Försoningen*, pp. 94 f., 97. Here is a point at which Billing rejects the orthodox Lutheran interpretation. In their work on the doctrine of the atonement, Aulén and Nygren continued further on this line during the 1930's.

88. *Ibid.*, p. 95. The main point of the quotation is that mercy and righteousness are now again *one*, as in classical prophetism. But now they are one in one *individual*, Jesus, and in this individual's work with *individuals*. More will be said about the unity between judgment and grace in the following section, "Death and Resurrection."

89. According to Billing, if an ethical conception has such great "elasticity" that it can resolve the problems that arise in a new situation, it is a sign of the "soundness" and "validity" of this conception. In this context see *De etiska tankarna*, pp. 12 f. Obviously Billing means that the ethics of Israel has this "soundness," and that it has been manifested in various historical situations.

90. *Försoningen*, pp. 104, 94–98, with the characteristic restriction in the note on p. 98.

91. See *ibid.*, pp. 24 f., 131–33.

92. Quotations from Billing's unpublished lecture, "Idealism och kristendom" (1934). See Gösta Wrede, *Kyrkosynen i Einar Billings teologi* (Stockholm, 1966), p. 122 n. 5. (According to the manuscript,

however, in the last line of the quotation we read "lärt," not "läst.")
It is typical of Billing that the word of resurrection comes out of the
great commission. Cf. Billing's sermon, "Från Emmaus till Jerusalem,"
*Gud's Närhet* (2nd ed.; Stockholm, 1949), pp. 68–70.

93. On Herrmann see *Försoningen*, pp. 104–8; on Kähler, *ibid.*, pp.
100 f.

94. Cf. Gustaf Aulén, "Einar Billings teologi," *Einar Billing in
memoriam* (Stockholm, 1940), pp. 59–66.

95. *Försoningen*, pp. 104 f.

96. See *De etiska tankarna*, pp. 183–85; *Försoningen*, pp. 22–24.
In both of these passages Billing rejects the idea that Paul, in a *literary*
sense, depended on Deutero-Isaiah in his interpretation of Jesus' death.

97. See especially *De etiska tankarna*, pp. 395, 409.

98. *Försoningen*, p. 78. "To this extent we could say that Jesus'
death was a sacrifice, not specifically demanded by God's retributive
righteousness, but rather by his people's perverted understanding of it."

99. Note the use of the word "history" in *Herdabrev*, pp. 54 f.

100. *I katekesundervisningens tjänst*, pp. 143 f.

101. *Försoningen*, p. 77.

102. See *Försoningen*, pp. 70–102; *I katekesundervisningens tjänst*,
pp. 95–98; *Herdabrev*, pp. 54–60.

103. This is true, e.g., of *The Living Word*, trans. Victor C. Pogue
(Philadelphia: Fortress Press, 1960) and of *Gospel and Church*, trans.
Ross Mackenzie (Philadelphia: Fortress Press, 1964). In these two
books together there are over fifty references to Einar Billing.

104. *Försoningen*, p. 91; cf. pp. 92–98, 128 f.

105. *Ibid.*, pp. 122 f.; *Herdabrev*, pp. 54 f. Reading Billing's exposition of these matters, one is easily reminded of a modern German
work, Jürgen Moltmann, *Theology of Hope*, trans. J. W. Leitch (New
York: Harper & Row, 1967), which is to a large extent based on an
interpretation of Exodus.

106. *Försoningen*, pp. 20, 23, 29 f., 48 f., 54 f., 57, 63–65, *et passim.*

107. See *De etiska tankarna*, pp. 105, 183–85, 369–71.

108. A start in this direction is to be found in *Försoningen*, pp. 62–
67, 132 f. In the first passage Billing refers to Rom. 6:1–8; Eph.
4:22–24; Col. 3:9–16; etc.

109. However, this New Testament material is discussed in Billing's
unpublished continuation of *De etiska tankarna*, a couple of manuscripts which unfortunately have not as yet been prepared for publication. See Wrede, *op. cit.*, pp. 310 f. These handwritten manuscripts are
difficult to interpret without an understanding of Billing's system of
abbreviation.

110. Something similar happens in my *Gospel and Church*. See the
index of that work, p. 264, on the word "imitation."

111. See *Our Calling*, p. 40; cf. p. 34, on "the cross."

112. *Luthers lära om staten* I, p. 87 f. and 187 f.; cf. *Our Calling*, p. 15.

113. Cf. again *I katekesundervisningens tjänst*, pp. 143 f.; also *Försoningen*, pp. 77, 124 f. Through the dispensation of the forgiveness of sins in the church "the historical Christ" has preserved his life as "forgiver."

114. *Guds närhet*, p. 70. The text was Luke 24:13–35, and Billing's beloved word was 24:33, "they rose that same hour."

115. Cf. *De etiska tankarna*, pp. 157 f.

116. *Ibid.*, pp. 164, 199.

117. *Ibid.*, p. 352.

118. *Försoningen*, pp. 100, 120. Billing's pattern anticipated that of Oscar Cullmann but had a stronger emphasis on forgiveness.

119. See *Den svenska folkkyrkan*, pp. 39 f.; also *Herdabrev*, p. 78. Cf. *I katekesundervisningens tjänst*, p. 146. The specific nature of the national church finds its clearest expression in the external form of *the territorial parish*.

120. Cf. Hans-Christoph Deppe, "Grundzüge der Geschichtstheologie bei Einar Billing," *Kerygma und Dogma* (1961), pp. 329 f.

121. *Försoningen*, p. 100.

122. *Den svenska folkkyrkan*, p. 132. This passage, which now is included in the second edition of *Den svenska folkkyrkan*, was originally a part of his lecture at the Pastoral Conference of 1937, which was published by itself in 1942. In this passage Billing could therefore look back on the breakthrough of his own conception of the church.

123. Note again the fundamental statement about Christ as now wandering "from nation to nation," *I katekesundervisningens tjänst*, pp. 143 f., and cf. also Wrede, *op. cit.*, pp. 158 f.

124. Billing frequently combines his own formulas of biblical theology with the special terms of the Reformation. See *Den svenska folkkyrkan*, p. 167.

# CHAPTER IV

# LUTHER
# AND THE GOSPEL

## 1. The Doctrine of the Two Realms

In his doctoral dissertation of 1900, Billing surprisingly often referred to Luther's principal theme, "the preaching of the gospel," in spite of the fact that his subject was Luther's teaching concerning the state. In the preface Billing explicitly formulated his fundamental problem in such a way that the *connection* between Luther's interpretation of the gospel and his ideas about the state became the central theme of his work. It was this connection that he proposed to elucidate:

The main question becomes then to what extent Luther's ideas about the state were connected with his interpretation of the gospel, or with the fundamental principles of his Reformation. It is of course true in general that Luther was not really a systematic theologian, but this does not mean that his thinking was confused and disorganized. This claim has often been made— too often, in fact—but it is remarkable that in more recent times such judgments have become less frequent. Instead we note a growing admiration for his logical consistency in what was for him the chief subject, the gospel. But this subject in reality governed *everything* that he wrote. This is what, with no conscious effort on his part, tied everything together into a united whole. . . . Only when we place Luther's ideas about the state in this frame of reference can we see them in their true historical context. Luther's historical significance was not that he suggested some more or less unrelated thoughts and paradoxes, but that for his time he was the preeminent preacher of the gospel.[1]

What Billing says here would probably not be challenged today by any competent person. But the way in which he developed in detail Luther's inner consistency proved to be his own inimitable achievement. Furthermore, our respect for Billing's ability to interpret Luther's thought increases as we note how carefully he recognized in the material elements that were contrary to his own interpretation. He declared frankly that in certain areas we have to abandon Luther's position. It will clarify matters if we first define some of the elements of Luther's teaching which Billing rejected. In doing this we will pay most attention to the elements connected with Luther's teaching about "the two realms."

Interpreters of Luther's so-called doctrine of the two realms agree that deeds done in "the earthly realm" are judged according to a quite external standard, which is a formal conformity to the law. But that standard suddenly proves to be inadequate "in heaven," before God, or "in conscience," as he sometimes expressed it. In the Kantian atmosphere which prevailed around the beginning of the twentieth century an external legality could hardly be conceived of as morality in the strict sense. But on *one* level, the "earthly," Luther approved of this rule of law. Yet, as we pointed out in the previous chapter, Billing's review of Israel's history showed an obviously negative attitude toward the concept of the *law*.[2] When "the law came in" it caused a derailment, and Israel's classical view became lost. Judaism, incapable of interpreting its own history, had substituted the pattern of retaliation for the living God. The law became "a substitute" for God.[3] Billing's negative attitude toward all legal terms appeared even in his dissertation on Luther of 1900. This negative attitude shows itself most clearly at a point which concerns not "the first use of the law" (an external standard here on earth), but rather "the second use of the law" (an accuser in conscience). According to Luther the law has a disciplinary, mortifying and crucifying, function to perform in the hearts of men.

Billing called this feature "Luther's ascetic point of view."[4] The enemy from whom Luther borrowed his terminology was the monastic piety, with its deliberate system of mortification. When Luther merely moved this mortification into man's daily life and interpreted "the cross" as a part of the earthly calling, said Billing, he also retained the medieval, negative, ascetic point of view. Billing plainly and clearly recognized Luther's unique conception of the *cross* in man's calling, but he just as clearly and plainly rejected it. He explained it as a medieval remnant.[5] Luther, too, from his experience as a monk had a doctrine of asceticism:

> He frequently returned to such thoughts in his writings. He, too, regarded asceticism as necessary, but no one had to search for it. The Christian's work in his calling provides him with the true means of asceticism. It is present in the trials and sufferings that come to the Christian, but it is present also in *work* itself. . . . He who takes his calling seriously will find how opposition and difficulties come from all directions. Here indeed everyone has received his due share of that *sudor vultus* which God in his wisdom has inflicted on men since the Fall. In comparison, all the mortifications of the monks are but playacting. The monks have tried in a cowardly fashion to escape from the bitter seriousness of real toil and self-denial. The Christian's work in his calling has indeed educative significance for his life, but only negatively. Luther could hardly go beyond that. . . . His point of view was, therefore, the natural result of his fundamental position. Yet it cannot be denied that something of a medieval dualism remained.[6]

This may well be so. But we should remember that the monasteries arose during the same fourth century in which Christianity became the religion of the state. This development made it possible to escape martyrdom, "the baptism of blood," which intermittently had occurred during the persecutions. Baptism was from the beginning a union with Christ in his death and resurrection (Rom. 6:3–8). When Christians could no longer recognize and experience the "cross" as realized in solidarity with Christ in worldly suffering before emperors and magistrates, they began instead to mortify the flesh in the monasteries and to invent artificial "crosses" for themselves. Luther's polemic against the monastic life returned "the cross" to the *worldly* environment. What of it if a remnant of "medieval asceticism" remained, as Billing says? Luther's doctrine of the calling was unquestionably altogether a doctrine of baptism, an interpretation of Romans 6:3 f. and of other similar texts in the letters of Paul. These are precisely the texts in the New Testament which Billing, in his analysis of Paul, left relatively unused.[7] In Billing's conception of the church, baptism was *infant* baptism, the sign of prevenient grace, God's election of us prior to any activity on our part.[8] When Billing rejected Luther's "medieval asceticism," there was danger that a biblical element would also get lost.

In Billing's thought, therefore, the two realms tended to become *one realm,* the kingdom where the forgiveness of sins was the sole governing principle.

> Anyone wishing to study Luther would indeed be in no peril of going astray were he to follow this rule: never believe that you have a correct understanding of a thought of Luther before you have succeeded in reducing it to a simple corollary of the thought of the forgiveness of sins. As examples from various viewpoints, we might point to his theory of the sacraments, his idea of the church, his doctrine of Christian liberty, and certainly also, to his teaching about the call.[9]

Billing naturally presented a correct picture of Luther's doctrine of the two realms, but he placed the picture in a secondary position. In his summary analysis the structure of the secular realm appeared as a medieval remnant. The whole emphasis fell on Luther's reconstruction of the spiritual realm, on the establishment of "the word," or "the gospel," or "the forgiveness of sins" (i.e., justification by faith), as the governing principle of the church. Such a reconstruction dissolved all the accepted material, even that which had at first been adopted from medievalism, the "ascetic" element which Billing from the beginning had regarded as decadent.[10] It becomes clear, therefore, how Billing could criticize Luther, reject a great part of his writings *and* nevertheless claim that he presented what Luther really had intended to say. This attitude is especially evident in *Our Calling (Vår kallelse)*, which is by far his most widely read book, having been translated into German, English, and Chinese.

A return to Luther, says Billing, is out of the question. "Of course, it is not merely a return to Luther, it cannot and may not be this."[11] There is one religious concept which Luther did not incorporate into his doctrine of the calling, but which we must now incorporate: the concept of "the kingdom of God." For Billing, furthermore, "the kingdom" is singular, one realm.[12] "In Luther's forgiveness of sins," said Billing, "there is virtually the idea of the kingdom of God." According to Luther, "the kingdom of God is nothing else than the actualization of the forgiveness of sins." It is not difficult to see how Billing in his stimulating analysis of Luther in *Our Calling* (1909) removed that element of Luther's doctrine which he had called "medieval," "ascetic," or "negative" in his doctoral thesis of 1900. Nor is it difficult to see how the forgiveness of sins became the center in Billing's new doctrine of the calling.[13] The center was obtained not from outside his tradition but from Luther himself. Billing maintained, for very good reasons, that forgiveness of sins was the very center of Luther's entire preaching of the *gospel*. He repeated this assertion in every one of his writings, no matter which sixteenth century subject was being discussed. The point of Billing's correction of Luther is clear and unambiguous: *the two realms tend to become one*. Billing held that what was essential in Luther had thereby been preserved over against one of the peripheral elements.

When one brings the two realms together into one, "the idea of forgiveness" becomes a very sophisticated concept. It was not so for Luther. For him the forgiveness of sins was the simple, easily understood word of absolution received in childlike faith. From this absolution man went out into the world, into the realm of the law "on this earth of work and the cross." Out there in the world were many complications with which man had to contend, even theologically. Such terms as "tending the office," "equitable," "freedom to do and to let," were means which Luther used in order to ease the transition from "the forgiveness of sins" to "the calling." These means built bridges between heaven and earth. But these terms of Luther played practically no role in Billing's work.[14] He published *Our Calling* in 1909, after both *The Ethical Thoughts* (*De etiska tankarna*; 1907) and *The Atonement* (*Försoningen*; 1908) had been published. He derived the content of the forgiveness of sins from the very complicated biblical theology which he had developed during the years 1907–8.

"In the forgiveness of sins we live through our exodus from Egypt." The *people* of Israel began *their* history with an exodus. The individual, however, had to wait for his "exodus" until Jesus came. Now he is here and meets us individually in the church. At that point the individual begins *his* history. The calling, which means everyday life and daily contingencies, constitutes history for every individual. This is Israel's history in miniature, filled with *God's mercy*, i.e., filled with grace and the forgiveness of sins, provided we are able to interpret the course of our life prophetically and "beat out its hidden gold." In this context, therefore, both suffering and the cross are really present in the life of the individual in a parallel to Israel's exile. But they are present in a different sense than they were in Luther. The material has been recast, reinterpreted, and incorporated into the one realm, the kingdom with the forgiveness of sins as the superior and dominant principle.[15] Billing's doctrine of the call was one of his many brilliant re-creations.

At this point a couple of extended quotations from *Our Calling* are in place.

> We might say that long before individuals could speak of a call as we have done, there existed a people, the people of Israel, who possessed a calling, exactly in the sense in which we have been using the word and in which Luther used it. Israel had received its calling through a powerful act of God's election or forgiveness, an act which, as we know, was ever in the thinking of Israel, namely, the exodus from Egypt, "out of the house of bondage." In this act lay also the assurance of a glorious goal which God had set for Israel, namely, he wanted to make it his people. The history that lay between this act and this goal included Israel's calling, and Israel knew beforehand that however contrary the appearances might seem, the ultimate purpose of its history was to come closer to God's goal, even as that history included ever new promises of God's grace toward his people. We know what a treasury of living and what a rich knowledge of God the prophets, the inspired interpreters of that history, were able to forge out of its stony materials. Indeed, thinking of the exile and Isaiah, we may say that the harder the materials the richer the prize. The prophets themselves never ceased to be amazed at the hidden riches of the ways of God. But the wealth of the knowledge they gained was nonetheless secondary to the constantly renewed confirmation of their basic conviction that God was living and near at hand. Everything is included in this one simple fact.[16]

If Israel's history can be said to include "a calling" of the people in Luther's sense, each one of us also lives through the whole of Israel's history in our calling.

> In the forgiveness of sins we live through our exodus from Egypt. Through it we become certain that God wants to lead us into his eternal kingdom. We know that whatever be the experiences we shall meet on the way, the innermost meaning of all of them is to bring us closer to the goal, and within all of them will be found a new message of grace. Just as the prophets beat hidden gold out of their people's history, so each of us must do with our own little history. If we could only learn faithfully and patiently to let the

forgiveness of sins discover to us our calling and let our calling
bring us back to forgiveness, we might also live through a Baby-
lonian Captivity where all hope seems lost, but wherein un-
dreamed of riches spring forth from the darkest hours.[17]

When Billing had arrived at this point in his theological
analysis, he could not proceed any further. Here began the
individual's own life, where such eventualities as items in a
diary, a letter to a friend, prayers, etc., occur. "We may abandon the theological discussion of the question without any
qualms, for there is no question that the matter is a live issue
for every individual," as I once suggested in an earlier
writing.[18] These subtle ideas about the individual's calling as
a miniature of Israel's history were not developed further in
Billing's later literary production.

But some of it *could* have been developed. *Our Calling* was
published in the year of "the great general strike," the only
general strike in Swedish history. In this book of 1909 Billing
discussed in passing the labor movement and its relationship
to the idea of the calling.

> I am convinced that if the church had not lost so much of the
> meaning of the gospel of the call, it would not have limited itself
> to a mere exhortation to workers to be content with their "calling."
> It would have been forced to see that back of the struggle for the
> raising of the condition of their class there was concealed a God-
> given call to the workers. And if the church had been able to
> couple with this idea of struggle the gospel of forgiveness of sins,
> how wholly different this struggle might have become! To us now
> the idea seems fantastically bold. But would it have seemed so, if,
> like Jesus, we had always been filled with the assurance of a living
> God, who ever creates anew, who "is working still"? That the
> church did not so succeed depends, as in the case of the indi-
> vidual, not primarily on a lack of understanding of the times, or
> the like, but on a lack of faith in the forgiveness of sins.[19]

As early as the school year 1908–9 Einar Billing, recently
appointed full professor, had lectured at Uppsala University
on the burning question, "Ethical Problems in the Modern

Labor Movement" ("De etiska problemen i den moderna arbetarfrågan").[20] The line from the social ethics of the Old Testament prophetism to the problems of labor was relatively simple and direct. The unity of righteousness and mercy, God's active presence in "history," that is, in the *present* and *its* contemporary social conflicts, etc.—all of this was relevant to this subject.[21] In this area there would have been a number of possibilities for developing Billing's biblical theology in the direction of *social ethics*.[22]

But Billing never published these lectures on the labor problem. Instead he produced other writings on different subjects, defending the organizational form of the Swedish national church against the attacks of the free churches. These were published and widely read. In this struggle Billing used Luther without revision—without making such revisions as he felt necessary in respect to Luther's doctrine of the call. There is in Luther a massive and naïve systematic structure which affects almost all of his readers. Perhaps one falls victim to this magnificent structure most easily when caught in a *polemical situation*. This is what happened to Billing. Around 1910 he lived in a milieu in which, for example, Luther's preface to *Deutsche Messe* was used by Waldenström and other free church leaders to support ideas of church discipline which were undoubtedly foreign to Luther and which had their roots in "enthusiastic" movements of the nineteenth and earlier centuries. These were movements which Luther had opposed.[23] Billing correctly affirmed that Luther regarded "the word," the preaching of the gospel, as the foundation of the church. As early as his dissertation of 1900, Billing had established this central point as the most specific characteristic of Luther. This is what had broken down medievalism (although certain medieval, "ascetic" remnants remained in his writings, as, for example, in the doctrine of the calling.)[24] In his struggle with the free churches Billing naïvely made use of Luther's

own language, which he did *not* do in his sophisticated argu-
mentation about the calling and in his social ethics.

We must pause at this important point in our analysis of
Einar Billing's theology. What does it *mean* in a debate about
the formal organization of the church to use Luther's own
language, his simple affirmations about the gospel as the
foundation of the church? If one keeps the conception of the
two realms clearly in mind, the law and the world will ultimately come in at their proper place, keeping the balance
intact. But what does it mean to use Luther's language in
reference to the church by itself if one has begun to reduce
the two realms to *one,* the kingdom with the forgiveness of
sins as the sole governing principle? From 1900 to 1909
Billing had carried on this reconstruction. How can a balance
then be achieved? The law can never be either seen or heard.
If one begins to modify Luther's usage, one must also modify
it in relation to the church. In that case one has to insert a
"demand" somewhere in the conception of the church; otherwise Luther's typical balance will be lost. In brief, the danger
is that one silently passes by the demand, and at the same
time with equal silence assumes with Luther that God's law
remains active on earth through the secular powers. In respect
to a national church that, like the Church of Sweden, is connected with the state, *silence about the law* easily becomes
fatal. Luther can be lost even when one quotes long sections
about the forgiveness of sins verbatim.

It is impossible to distinguish the words and acts for which
Einar Billing the public official is responsible from the words
and expressions which Einar Billing the author has published.
What a bishop says in his Cathedral Chapter and in the Diet
of the Church belongs to the public and operates with the same
power that a published book does. In a small country like
Sweden, it has perhaps even greater influence. Billing lived
in a church whose ordinances and official documents were

promulgated by the government and whose income came by way of a tax collecting agency. He never, during his whole official ministry, did anything to break this connection with the state or to limit the state's power over "the law" in the church. In his *Pastoral Letter (Herdabrev)* he maintained instead that this order of affairs was good and ought to be continued.[25] The point at which the old order was *broken up* through Billing's energetic initiative was, typically enough, the point at which the *individual* and his conscience had to be safeguarded. The old state-church arrangement was to remain as long as possible, but the individual must be given freedom to withdraw from the national church if he so desired.[26] As we have already remarked, Billing carried through his complicated conception of forgiveness and his conception of history in his biblical theology in reference to the *individual*. But as soon as he dealt with *the official form of organization* in the national church he directly appropriated and repeated Luther's less complicated utterances about the forgiveness of sins, with the polemical point directed toward the free churches.

The term, "the forgiveness of sins," functioned therefore in two radically different contexts in Billing's theology. In meditations, sermons, and edifying addresses he spoke to the individual and showed him that which is available personally in the forgiveness of sins. His variations on this theme were endless. He could never fully express his amazement:

> Whoever has any inkling of the meaning of the forgiveness of sins knows that a whole lifetime will not be sufficient for a full understanding of it. For each new experience makes us feel that we had no understanding of it at all before.[27]

These variations on the theme were played in *Our Calling*, in the central parts of *The Communion of Saints (De heligas gemenskap)*, and in the older parts of *The Swedish National Church (Den svenska folkkyrkan)*.[28] The language of these writings stems from that used in *The Ethical Thoughts* and in *The Atonement.* The individual's life is "a history," and gift and responsibility are intertwined.

But the offer of grace and the demand inherent in this gift *fell apart* in another set of Billing's works, that is, when he spoke about the organizational form of the national church. Then the external form of the national church was an expression of the proffered *grace.* The demand in the law could not appear in the organization itself (the territorial parish); it had to find other means of expression (through what was said in the territorial parishes by way of education and nurture).[29] Alongside the parish church stood the free church chapel or the mission house with a different pattern of organization. These had an external form which emphasized the biblical demand for commitment.[30] This kind of discussion Billing carried on especially in the later parts of *The Swedish National Church,* where he directly recommended certain solutions to problems in regard to the church law.[31] The language in these sections often comes directly and unchanged from Luther's writings about "the spiritual government." But he took only half of Luther, the half that dealt with the gospel and the church. The law was left out.

None of Billing's heirs in Sweden continues his meditative, varied, and inexhaustible address to the individual about the forgiveness of sins. But there are some trained in church law, experienced in contact with lawyers and state officials—we might describe them as administrators—who continue Billing's formulations in the area of organization: the official order of the national church is an expression of prevenient grace, "the forgiveness of sins offered to the people of Sweden." This one-sided preservation of the heritage from Billing causes a certain dilution of the conception of the national church in Sweden. The term "national church" *(folkkyrka)* becomes more and more impoverished, without personal appeal. The zeal for the

individual and his welfare seems rather to be at home among
the opponents of the national church.

The order to be pursued now in this chapter on Luther and
the gospel is self-evident. We must deal first with Billing's use
of the phrase, "the forgiveness of sins," and thereafter with
the territorial parish and the individual.

### 2. The Forgiveness of Sins

Billing was not very interested in the young Luther. There
are some indications that he wanted to place "the breakthrough of the Reformation" later in Luther's life, possibly as
late as 1520.[32] The Reformation did not break through until
Luther had attained to full insight concerning the message of
the *forgiveness of sins,* or until the *word* clearly became the
means of grace.[33]

> The word received its dominant place when it became clear that
> grace is gospel, "the forgiveness of sins," and thereby also "life
> and salvation." The word is a means of grace only because it pro-
> claims the gospel. It even *is* the gospel. "The word" and "the
> gospel" were interchangeable concepts, as far as Luther was con-
> cerned. Luther could just as well have said that the gospel was its
> own means of grace. The word, in its essential meaning, meets the
> Christian in two forms: in the Holy Scriptures and in preaching.
> Both find an entirely new place in the Christian's life. The Bible
> is no longer "a book of law which contains much good teaching."
> This is a misunderstanding which has always been the result of
> the confusion of law and gospel. The word is preeminently a
> means of grace, the point where the Christian directly meets his
> Lord Christ, a spring from which he draws forgiveness, life, and
> salvation. . . . One could say that only through the gospel has
> the Bible now become differentiated from all human books of law
> and teaching. But what is its relationship to the sermon, to the
> proclamation in the church? It is the norm of the sermon, and, at
> least indirectly, its source. But, from the point of view of its value
> for the Christian, "the sermon" has full parity with it; *yes, from
> a certain point of view it is even superior to the biblical word.*[34]

Luther's strong emphasis on the sacramental character of
the spoken word has been frequently noted in recent Swedish

research. In his dissertation, *The Function of the Sermon (Predikans uppgift)*, Henrik Ivarsson described the function of the sermon—to "administer" grace—with a precision never before attained. Ivarsson succeeded in his task because of his constant comparison of Luther's work with pietistic preaching.[35] It is obvious that there is to be found in Luther a specific concentration on the preacher's duty to *confer* the forgiveness of sins on the congregation gathered for worship. He has to distribute this gift to them in essentially the same way as he distributes the bread and the wine.

Billing was therefore in complete agreement with Luther when he continually returned to the one point, the forgiveness of sins. But Billing gave the phrase a specific and individual touch, which is quite modern, and foreign to the sixteenth century. The central point is the personal growth and maturity of the individual as he lives his life in the frictions of daily tasks and constantly returns to "the forgiveness of sins" morning and evening. *The Communion of Saints,* more than any other of his published works, permits us an insight into Billing's personal life. He held that in our intercourse with our fellowmen we find ourselves "in an intermediate area between the great history and the individual's purely personal life."[36] Every time we think of what could have resulted from our association with others, our own guilt becomes clear. But the gift remains in the midst of our guilt and our consciousness of failure. In the morning we read in the paper about the crime of a man who has failed morally. Everyone who is even slightly aware of the nature of guilt realizes with trepidation how close he could have been to becoming a criminal. He thanks God for all the people who "stood watch": father, mother, spouse, brothers and sisters, children, teachers, and friends—"and in addition a great crowd of known and unknown, living and long since dead." This is the communion of saints, filled with God's mercy toward us, filled with the forgiveness of sins.[37]

In the evening prayers we look back on the failures of the day; new failures, new people whom we, like the priest and the Levite, have "passed by" (Luke 10:31 f.). If we look back on the day with the certainty of the forgiveness of sins, all our failures are wiped out as soon as we lift them up into the presence of God. "While we are still praying," God at once bids us to return to the person we passed by. As we pray we begin to seek out our fellowmen one after another in intercession.[38] The communion of saints and all its everyday duties emerge out of the forgiveness of sins. But prayer, which is fundamentally individual, suddenly and frequently becomes for Billing most universal, "the great history" in which all the dead, all the young, and all the coming generations belong. It becomes a thanksgiving for all those who "stood watch" over us, and an intercession for those who after us will sojourn here and be tempted. The parish pastor's prayer for his territorial parish, the bishop's prayer for his diocese, prayers offered with the church register and the diocesan parish list open, appeared to Billing as exceedingly significant.[39] The individual is an individual precisely when he knows himself as inseparably connected with the many.[40] As soon as Billing pronounced the three words, "forgiveness of sins," he associated with them this whole wide world, and he assumed that this comprehensive content of the conception conformed to Luther's thought.

Whoever knows Luther, even but partially, knows that his various thoughts do not lie alongside each other, like pearls on a string, held together only by common authority or perchance by a line of logical argument, but that they all, as tightly as the petals of a rosebud, adhere to a common center, and radiate out like the rays of the sun from *one* glowing core, namely, the gospel of the forgiveness of sins. . . . We could take all of them in order and say something like this: the church is the forgiveness of sins, the sacraments are the forgiveness of sins, liberty is the forgiveness of sins, the call is the forgiveness of sins.[41]

Billing noted accurately that Luther's teaching about the state was essentially *ethics*. "It is not meant to be anything but a chapter in ethics." Billing adds that in reality it was a chapter in *individual*, rather than social, ethics.[42] This is an excellent observation and reflects Luther's thought accurately. The doctrine of the secular realm concerns the *call* directed to each and every person. Billing combined Luther's visible manifestation of the law with the visible manifestation of prevenient grace in the parish church—in the building itself and in its furniture, in the bells, in the baptismal font, etc. As the previous quotation indicates, he gathered everything under the forgiveness of sins: "the church is the forgiveness of sins, . . . the call is the forgiveness of sins."[43] Naturally, Billing changed the frame of reference when he dissolved the sixteenth century's rigid contrast between law and gospel and combined the two realms into one. But even within this new frame of reference there was room for correctly reproduced features of Luther's views (the prominence of absolution, the individualistic character of the ideas concerning the state, etc.). He did not change the frame of reference in an arbitrary manner. He cited reasons for his changes, and, most important, he kept another frame at hand. This was his view of history, a frame of reference based on his biblical theology in which the material derived quite faithfully from Luther easily found a place.

Even in the frame of reference based on his biblical theology the central element was the forgiveness of sins. It was of course to the individual and not to the nation that Jesus provided this exodus from Egypt. But the individual continued to live *Israel's* life. The individual, like Israel of old, "searched" for "a fact to which he could attach the idea of grace."[44] When Israel could not find such a fact in the present, the election became imprisoned in the past, while the present was dominated by law and retribution—and by a mild indulgence.[45] If faith is to receive sustenance and persist, the external history in which man lives in the present must contain works of God's mercy. After the biblical texts had been written and gathered, when the gospel of the forgiveness of sins was being proclaimed orally in Europe, the question about the continuance of the idea of pure grace in Europe was the same as the following question: Where in the individual European's life can there be found "a fact to which the idea of grace can be attached"? Where can an external act reach him with a reminder of God's mercy that is new every morning?

Billing's answer to this question was surprisingly trivial. It was as prosaic as the list of parishes in front of the bishop as he prayed. All people, all individuals in this European world, have "a fact to which they can attach the idea of grace." This "fact" is the parishes, the church buildings, the baptismal fonts, the peal of the church bells early and late.[46] Billing is the only theologian I know of who built a theology on this unique artifact of the European system, the parishes.

Regin Prenter, in a rather unusual medium, the 1949 *Yearbook of the Diocese of Viborg (Viborgs stifts årbog)* very skillfully wrested from Billing's hand the argument concerning "church order" taken from Luther, and turned it against the very heart of the conception of the Swedish national church. If the official church organization is *free,* as Billing in conformity with Luther always asserted, this external order of parishes and territorial churches cannot be anything but "a civil establishment." This was Grundtvig's term for the Danish parish organization and for the whole external structure of the national church. According to Prenter, Grundtvig was closer to agreement with Luther than was Billing.[47] Prenter thought that Billing had gone astray because of his polemic against the free churches in Sweden.[48] Since his opponents advocated a certain external form of organization on the basis of the Bible, a free church with individual and voluntary membership, Billing was forced to base *his* external form of the parish with

geographical boundaries on the Bible also. But neither one
is really biblical. The only criteria in matters of order are
"expediency and adequacy."

We have already sought in a different way to substantiate
what Prenter's criticism implied. If it is assumed that the New
Testament demand for commitment can lead to a free church
type of organization, but that the highest principle, the concept of grace, demands the territorial parish, then in the very
*organization* of the church demand and grace have become
separated. In that case Billing's typical unity of righteousness
and mercy, judgment and grace, has been dissolved. But the
split pertains only to the external organization.[49] There are no
parishes without individuals. As soon as the individual comes
into view, Billing's writings become much more weighty and
vital than his official utterances in the Diet of the Church.
Billing's "individual" has his whole personal history: his everyday activity, his worship, his temptations, and his prayers.
Nothing is missing. We misinterpret Billing's conception of
the national church if we do not keep it in line with all the
rest that he untiringly tried to impress upon the individual in
regard to the significance of the forgiveness of sins for *him*
individually.[50]

The territorial parishes indeed mean, to use a phrase well
known in Sweden, "the forgiveness of sins to the people of
Sweden." But within the geographical boundaries of these
parishes dwell nothing but individuals.

### 3. The Territorial Parish and the Individual

According to Billing it is not the people who constitute the
primarily active and creative element in the national church.
He became, therefore, greatly alarmed when some in Germany
during the 1930's began to use *Volk* and *Volkskirche* in such
a way that the people, rather than the gospel, became primary
and normative.

What the result will be if one deliberately and consistently follows this tendency becomes apparent if we observe what is taking place in our great neighboring country to the south. When I have read theological attempts to justify this ideal of a national church, I have often winced as from the crack of a whip. I have done so especially when the arguments have sometimes been condensed into a slogan that deceptively reminds us of our own old watchword: Sweden's people—God's people. A tendency in that direction, least of all in the direction of making our people a privileged people above all others, has never been in our minds at all—this we can unhesitatingly affirm. But for a church that has learned to love this inclusive form of organization which embraces all the people, the temptation lies near at hand, nearer even than we suspect, to go at least a little in that direction. In order to find room for all and preserve points of contact with all, we may be tempted to discount a little of the religious character of the message and be satisfied with an external universality. We may do so even though it cannot be supported by, or may even stand in opposition to, the inner universality of the gospel message.[51]

This utterance was not merely a rejection of the power of the people in the church as advocated by National Socialism. As Billing went on, he directed his criticism also to Sweden and to Swedish "national churchmanship."

Since the theme of our study is Billing and his influence, it is not our task here to trace later deviations in Swedish thinking regarding the national church. The frequent use of the title, "theologian of the national church," by the daily press and other mass media has really nothing to do with Billing. Since it seems that the adjective "national" (= *folk* = people) is the term that misleads, I think it would be better in analyzing Billing's conception of the church to employ the phrase, *the territorial parishes,* and to avoid, if possible, the ambiguous designation "national" *(folk).* Billing maintained that if the starting point is prevenient grace or, in other words, the gospel, one arrives directly at "the national church or, *even more precisely,* at the territorial parishes."[52] This statement (at the 1929 Diet of the Church) implies that the phrase, "the territorial parishes," is a more definitive and precise expression of the grace of God than "the national church." It will serve as a guide for us here as we examine Billing's conception of the church. On the one hand we have the territorial parishes ("all," or at least "the many"), and, on the other hand, the individual. It will become clear in our analysis that between these two there are both antithesis and coherence.

That Billing emphasized the territorial parish and not the people was due to the character of God's grace as *action*. If one were looking for a visible and audible manifestation of God's merciful approach to Sweden's people, "a fact to which the idea of grace could be attached," one could hardly find any evidence of it on the national scene.[53] But every parish has "a fact," the church building itself. Since the whole of Sweden is divided up into territorial parishes, and since no section of its area lies outside the sphere of the responsibility and activity of these many church edifices, the people as a whole are sought by Christ as he in "the word" comes wandering "from nation to nation."[54] The primary focus, in Billing's view, was the territorial parish, the secondary was the people. He started in "the parish movement" which J. A. Eklund and others had inaugurated in Sweden. The purpose of this movement was to create new life in the local parishes by new forms of activity. At about the turn of the century this movement had achieved some great results in the church, not least in the Uppsala area.[55]

In order to understand the significance of the idea that the territorial parish by its very *organization* becomes a bearer of God's grace, it is necessary to include the *individual* from the start. In the free church organization the congregation must be established on the basis of the individual's conversion and commitment. In principle, one becomes a Christian first and then later becomes a member of the congregation. The congregation consists of believing persons who seek membership on the basis of possessing a faith attained prior to membership in the *ecclesia*. In the territorial congregation, on the other hand, the individual awakens in a room where God's grace has been active even before the individual has attempted to do anything at all. But grace is not just active in general, it has already reached the *individual,* embraced him within the *ecclesia* prior to all his decisions and commitments. Grace literally comes "before" faith. It is "prevenient grace."[56] Naturally, infant baptism reveals this prevenient grace most clearly. In baptism one individual at a time, as his name is called, becomes a member of the church of Christ. As we have emphasized already, Billing's theology was a theology of infant baptism.

> I will also indicate the birthday of the national church. As far as I can see, it began when for the first time a child was baptized in a Christian family. This very likely took place already in New Testament times. We see it clearly when Paul at one time reduces *ad absurdum* an argument that would have established too narrow limits for the congregation. He says: If we were to follow that principle the result would be that "your children would be unclean, but as it is they are holy." Why? Precisely because God's call includes them also. This is what people have sensed. God has beforehand made provision for the children. They are already under the influence of his word and the gospel. The parents simply recognize this fact and thank God for it, as they baptize their children. And I wonder if at the first infant baptism they did not already think of how Jesus blessed the children, even though nothing is said directly in that passage about baptism.[57]

Everything, moreover, in the structure of the territorial parish is related to infant baptism. The voice of the church bells calls every individual. Every individual's name is recorded in the church register. Even the church building itself, the parish church, belongs to all. It is their building; they are at home in it.[58] That the parish has a *geographical* boundary, that one can point to the line, to a certain ditch, or to the edge of the forest—these most commonplace features are the deepest spiritual element in the territorial parish. God's love is present in such an earthly way that not even a small piece of land remains outside of his presence. Every square inch is a part of the territorial parish.[59] The national church is therefore the bearer of the forgiveness of sins to all people living on the soil that is divided by parish boundaries.

> Not all seek God, at least not consciously, but he seeks them all. He began to seek them long before they were able to seek him, and he does not desist because they fail. His forgiveness stands waiting for even the one who has gone farthest astray. But even the one who has gone farthest on the way to return home has nothing to depend on but the same unmerited forgiveness. They are all sinners whom God never tires of forgiving, all "these non-descript crowds between the geographical fences."[60]

The term "fences" at the end of the quotation was taken from a sarcastic speech about "the state church" by P. Waldenström at the 1908 Diet of the Church.[61] Typically, Billing quietly picked up all these scoffing words and transformed them into excellent expressions of the gospel. He made them honorable words, expressive of the incarnation.

If, however, all within the territorial parish are equal before God, and if their fellowship with God depends entirely on forgiveness, the result is not monotonous uniformity. Every person is an individual and has *his own* history. Furthermore, the local parish in the Swedish church, to which Billing belonged and which he described, is a most democratic institution. It was in a sense the source of Swedish democracy and provided relatively wide opportunities for individual initiative. (On the national and diocesan levels, democracy was less in evidence.) Billing defined carefully the individual differences, such as circles and fellowships, *within* the territorial parishes. He welcomed "the mobilizing of the laity for greater activity in the church," and he expected a greater manifestation of private initiative in the future. (This has of course actually come true since the mid-twentieth century.)[62] But the really effective jolt to the territorial parish was supplied by Billing himself in his motion introduced in the 1929 Diet of the Church, relative to "the freedom to withdraw." As a result, the *individual* found radical possibilities of dissolving the uniform system of church government which up to that time had characterized Lutheranism. The modern pluralistic situation was born.

There was something prophetic in Billing's stubborn defense of the freedom of the individual. The political situation in Sweden around the year 1929 was such that the state was not positively interested in extending religious freedom. After 1932 the Social Democratic regime decided what measures the state was to undertake, and it was this party's timetable that determined in what order the problems were to be handled. On that timetable, social problems had priority, and cultural problems, including the problems of the churches, were secondary. Consequently, it was not until 1951 that the new law of religious freedom advocated by Billing was passed. The law went into effect on January 1, 1952.[63] Billing, however, had insisted all along that the *church* itself should take the initiative regarding the individual's privilege of free withdrawal, especially when the state was passive, uninterested, and indifferent toward religious freedom. He asserted in 1929 that "the problem can never come at a time more advantageous for the church than just now."[64] What Billing feared most of all was that the initiative for the individual's religious freedom would come from the state and be forced on the church at a time when the church, without insight into its own inner nature, would only reluctantly accept such freedom for the individual. In that case the church would represent coercion, "law," and the state would represent freedom for the individual. But this would be a false stance for a church that was to be the exodus out of Egypt for every individual!

Here, as in everything else, Billing was mostly concerned
with "the purity of the gospel." "According to my way of
thinking, the religious task of the church demands a consistent
and thoroughgoing principle of freedom."[65] We have already
noted that Billing interpreted the significance of the forgiveness of sins in two different "languages," or two different
patterns. The one belonged to the Reformation. It was the
language of "the spiritual government" which Billing used
without much reformulation in his pleading for a certain
ecclesiastical *organization,* the pattern of the national church.
This pattern expressed the gospel's universal offer of grace to
all, but it was difficult to express within this pattern the demand inherent in the gift. Gift and response, *Gabe und Auf-
gabe,* tended to fall apart into two types of organization, the
national church and the free churches. The other language was
Billing's original creation and appeared in his works on
biblical theology in 1907 and in 1908. In this pattern, gift
and demand went together. Righteousness and mercy, judgment and grace, were *one,* as in Israel.[66] He employed this
language whenever he spoke to *individuals,* to students in
summer conferences, to worshiping congregations. Here the
accent was always on the unity of faith and the secular world,
always from the point of view of individual "history." In view
of these two patterns it is not possible to say unequivocally
that Billing's proposed law guaranteeing freedom to withdraw
from the church would safeguard the interest in the individual
which was inherent in his biblical theology as that stands in
contrast to his Reformation concern for "the spiritual government," the government by the gospel.

In a certain sense, peculiarly enough, the very opposite
happened. Luther's writings contain an abundance of passages
which assert the need of *freedom* for faith. These passages
sound very modern, and they are filled with anger against
all forms of coercion in spiritual matters. Luther's own per-

sonal experience as a young exegete of the Bible in the monastery shines through here. He found material in the Bible which was to shake the authorities of all times, the spiritual and the secular alike. With a consistency unusual in history he determined that his weapon was to be the spoken and written word, nothing else. In his total and mature world view, therefore, law, coercion, and violence belonged entirely to the sphere of the secular government. The church had to be governed by the gospel, the free offer of grace to all.[67] This broad view of Luther determined Einar Billing's outlook. His proposal of 1929 did not really imply a change in this respect. In order that it might become perfectly clear that the free offer of the gospel to every man governs the church in Sweden, every individual who so desires must have the right to sever his ties with the church freely and unconditionally.[68] What was abolished here was only the unity between church and state which Lutheran orthodoxy had enforced by law. What was established, we could say on the other hand, was the pluralistic city of Wittenberg around 1520, where one could have met all kinds of confessions on the streets, freely speaking to one another and against one another. Only in a situation of that kind can it become clear that the *word* is the foundation of the church.[69]

Even though Billing felt that he conformed to Luther when he urged that the individual be given the right to withdraw, it was in a real sense certainly the unique work of Jesus as reported in the New Testament that was the decisive factor. Luther was, after all, nothing but an interpreter of the old gospel in the specific context of the sixteenth century. According to the four Gospels, Jesus gave the forgiveness of sins to individuals tormented by the law. But on the basis of this early Christian pattern it is not possible to discern a solicitude for the individual that might be expressed in this negative "withdrawal from the church." By use of the word "withdrawal" we have already posited the existence of a territorial parish that includes everyone living within its borders. We have then presupposed the medieval parochial system, which was unknown in and would have been incomprehensible to the pre-Constantine era.[70] I am wondering if we do not find here a really progressive element in Einar Billing. The dissolution of the European state churches and the advance of pluralism will evidently proceed in two acts. Each act presents its own problems. Sweden is as yet only in the first act.

There was a time in Europe when Christian congregations were simply geographical entities whose borders could be clearly marked. Some rebel groups with their own acts of baptism and tables for communion tried, of course, to oppose the system, but as a general rule they were severely suppressed by the secular authorities, whose police powers served to protect the national churches, or the territorial parishes. These rebels have now in turn become established free churches and can expect the protection of the secular law if they are disturbed in their worship. The bastions and privileges of the national churches in the secular order are slowly crumbling away and soon will be nothing but ruins. In this situation the national churches will become free churches, separated from the state. Present-day theology, especially that of Karl Barth, accepts this development and presents cogent arguments why the churches themselves should positively participate in this crumbling process. The Barthian doctrine of baptism, for example, belongs in this context, and so do the criticism of the classical doctrine of "natural law," the neglect of the doctrine of creation, and several other features. In this first act the national churches gladly accept the old pattern of the free churches without being aware that the old territorial parishes preserved an essentially *Christian* element, an element which the free churches in their revolt have neglected from the beginning.

After the close of the nineteenth century, Einar Billing helped to usher the rigid Swedish state church into this new pluralistic era, and he did so from the center of the *gospel.* This was the significance of the important proposal of 1929.[71] The first act has not yet been played out in Sweden.

Today in international theological literature we can already hear the introductory notes of the music to the second act. This second act begins in earnest when every existing church is a free church, when no Christian parish any longer has geographical boundaries, and when membership in the church depends entirely on personal decision. I am a Christian, I choose to become a member. *Thus we begin to discover what was lost when the territorial parish was dissolved.* So far it is most noticeable in the connotations of the words as we speak of "church" and "world." The word "church" tends to acquire a negative connotation, while "world" becomes positive. Outside the narrow confines of the congregation, outside of this group of voluntary adherents, that is, out in "the world," one discovers creative powers which cannot have come from any source other than Christ. In our time, it is said, the church ought "to follow the world." The world is ahead of the church in following Christ, not vice versa.[72] How is it possible to contrive such a point of view? It is possible in *one* particular way. In the first act the conception of the church became constricted. After this constriction "the church" became identical with a small, compact clique, while all the rest within the common geographical boundaries was called "the world." In the second act it suddenly becomes evident that "the world" stands closer to Christ.

This *discovery,* which now appears as something new, is from one point of view what the old parish church preached, as Billing saw it even before the First World War. This is his most profound and prophetic point. Here stands a *house* which speaks, a *building,* not a religious person. Men make "decisions," they are sectarian, they establish boundaries where there ought to be none.[73] It is only the church building itself that understands what the gospel proposes to do with men.

> Here I stand, it says, and throughout all the centuries I have Sunday after Sunday let the bells ring out their invitation to all who are weary and heavy laden to come to me. I have been glad for every one who has come; but most of all I have rejoiced when one came whom I had thought was gone forever. Then it seemed to me I heard the song of the angels join the peal of the bells. There has indeed been an inscription over the entrance to this church: Let every one who calls on the name of the Lord depart from unrighteousness. Perhaps it was not always as clear as it ought to have been, but I believe no one who came failed to notice it. *But yet I have never put a guard at the door to stop those who came, or to ask them about their rights to be there.* Those who wanted to could come before God on their own responsibility and take what they wanted. Who are you that ask others about their rights? Have you perchance received some other kind of right besides this, that you are a sinner whom God never wearies of forgiving? *No one can without peril evade the proclamation of the old parish church.* But what I wanted most to emphasize was that the minister himself needs to listen to it for the sake of *his own* preaching. There are those who regard it as a very enviable thing when a minister can speak to a congregation whose members have attached themselves to him personally without reference to any other reasons. They may have joined him because of the similarity between his and their spiritual life, or because of their appreciation of his religious personality. For myself I must confess that I cannot think of anything more terrifying.[74]

This territorial parish which Billing had in mind had room for a great deal of what we now call "the world," but which he from the beginning was wise enough to call "the church." When in *The Communion of Saints* he enumerated those who "stood watch" over us, he included those who did not profess faith in God but who through their rigid demand for righteousness "pointed out for you the way to God, so that now you understand better than they did how close God was to them."[75] Billing's terminology appears more cogent than the modern reasoning, according to which "the world" follows Christ, while "the church" does not.

But it is only from one point of view that Billing agrees with what the modern secularizing theologians say. At another point he departs from them, and at that point he surpasses them. The modern talk about "the world" as the sphere in which Christ works is *moralistic*. In its social concerns and acts the world is better than the church. But in Billing's thought it was the gospel of *the forgiveness of sins* which the parish church proclaimed to all who came near it day after day. The church building is an action directed toward the community. It is not, however, just any kind of action, but an act of *election,* "a fact to which the idea of grace can be attached."[76]

It is utopian to imagine that Europe can return to the pre-Constantine situation. *One* factor which was absent before Constantine—the parish churches scattered over our whole continent—will remain. They remind us of the old parochial system, which was not established in Africa, Asia, and America. It is and will remain typically European. In many instances these houses of worship are the most notable buildings in the community from the point of view of both architecture and art. Furthermore, they are usually built of stone, and thus even from that point of view they are permanent. They will stand as remnants of the Constantine era long after confessing Christians have become minorities in all of Europe. What does their continued presence have to say?

They do not proclaim a moralistic message that "the world" is better than "the church." Nor are they moralistic witnesses to the effect that "the church" is better than "the world." In reality, they are not saying anything about one group of people over against others. No, they bear witness to *the God who acts*; they speak about him who seeks *all*. In its totality Billing's theology was an interpretation of the message of these parish churches to the people of Europe.[77] It would not be surprising if, after the relative de-Christianization of Europe, his interpretation would appear more relevant and modern than it does today. Then also the care of these churches for the *individual*, every individual who seeks shelter in them, will appear in a new light. The number of buildings which are available to *every* individual, and which provide for him exit, exodus, a gospel, will probably not be very great.

## NOTES TO CHAPTER IV

1. Einar Billing, *Luthers lära om staten* I (Uppsala, 1900), p. vii. Cf. also Billing's brief and popularly written book for the quadricentennial celebration of the Reformation, *Luthers storhet* (Uppsala, 1917), pp. 17–26.

2. Einar Billing, *De etiska tankarna i urkristendomen* (2nd ed. enlarged; Stockholm, 1936), pp. 167–71, 199–210.

3. *Ibid.,* pp. 157 f.; also, from a fundamental point of view, p. 7.

4. See *Luthers lära om staten* I, pp. 86–89.

5. Ibid., pp. 87, 188. Cf. Einar Billing, *Our Calling,* rev. trans. Conrad Bergendoff ("Facet Books – Social Ethics Series," 1; Philadelphia: Fortress Press, 1964), pp. 6, 34.

6. *Luthers lära om staten* I, pp. 86 f.

7. In *Försoningen* ([2nd ed.; Stockholm, 1921], pp. 64–67) Billing presents attempts at utilizing such passages in Paul, but they remain attempts. Cf. above, III:4, "Death and Resurrection."

8. Einar Billing, *Herdabrev till prästerskapet i Västerås stift* (2nd ed.; Stockholm, 1962), pp. 81–83; and *Den svenska folkkyrkan* (2nd ed.; Stockholm, 1963), p. 111. Cf. Gösta Wrede, *Kyrkosynen i Einar Billings teologi* (Stockholm, 1966), pp. 148 f., 155–57.

9. *Our Calling,* p. 4.

10. Cf. *Luthers lära om staten* I, pp. 159, 199, and again pp. 87, 188. The connection between the law and the secular government is emphasized especially in *Luthers lära om staten* III (unpublished manuscript).

11. *Our Calling,* p. 15.

12. The following two quotations are from *Our Calling,* p. 16.

13. *Ibid.,* pp. 5, 6, 8, 14, 42, *et passim.*

14. It is typical that Billing uses a term like "equitable" (Sw. *billighet*). But there is no correspondence to Luther's use of the same term, nor any relation to Luther's fundamental point of view. See, e.g., *De etiska tankarna*, pp. 216 f., and *Försoningen*, p. 95.

15. In this connection we should remind ourselves of the central place which *suffering* occupies in Billing's *De heligas gemenskap* (2nd ed.; Stockholm, 1943), pp. 19–24, 28 f., 41–43. Even in this book, which is perhaps the finest of his more personal writings, the forgiveness of sins is the constant theme.

16. *Our Calling*, p. 39. The parallel to *De etiska tankarna* is obvious throughout even in details, e.g., "Judaism" in the individual's life. Cf. *Our Calling*, pp. 20 f.

17. *Ibid.*, p. 40.

18. Cf. my *Gospel and Church*, trans. Ross Mackenzie (Philadelphia: Fortress Press, 1964), pp. 237 (especially n. 37) and 247 ff. (especially n. 24 on p. 249). The connection with Billing is obvious in both instances.

19. *Our Calling*, p. 42.

20. See Wrede, *op. cit.*, p. 19 n. 19. Very interesting is the manuscript, "Nationellt och socialt" (1914), now in the University Library in Lund, in which Billing discusses the relationship between the gospel and democracy, pp. 36–45.

21. Cf. *De etiska tankarna*, especially pp. 100–105.

22. It was on the initiative of Billing that the ecumenical meeting in Stockholm in 1925 proposed the establishment of an Institute for Social Ethics in Geneva. See Wrede, *op. cit.*, pp. 246 f.

23. See *Folkkyrkan och den frikyrkliga församlingsprincipen* (Uppsala, 1912), p. 93. Cf. Bengt Hallgren, *Kyrkotuktsfrågan* (Lund, 1963), p. 12.

24. *Luthers lära om staten* I, pp. vii, 74 f., 105, 199, 88 f., 187 f.

25. See *Herdabrev*, pp. 92–99; cf. Wrede, *op. cit.*, pp. 236–41, on the law and the state.

26. Suggestions along this line appear already in *Herdabrev* (1920), pp. 82 f., nine years prior to the Diet of the Church at which the motion was made.

27. *Our Calling*, p. 20. Cf. Einar Billing, *Den uppriktige och Gud* (2nd ed.; Uppsala, 1917), p. 23.

28. The literary form of these older parts, the meditations of a pastor in regard to his parish (pp. 12–49), continually suggests individual applications.

29. *Den svenska folkkyrkan*, pp. 53 f., 137 f.

30. According to Billing, however, the demand is not "the chief concern" (*ibid.*, p. 53) in the choice of *organization* of the church. The chief principle is the gospel—the gospel offered to all. Cf. *Herdabrev,* pp. 85–87.

31. In the second edition of *Den svenska folkkyrkan* (1963), both the long speech at the 1929 Diet of the Church (pp. 104–27) and the lecture at the 1937 Pastoral Conference about church and state (pp. 128–86) are included.

32. See "1517–1520," Billing's investigation of Luther's development (*Uppsala universitets årsskrift* [1917], pp. 13–15), with strong emphasis on the year 1520 (*De captivitate Babylonica*); also p. 82 with emphasis on the years 1521–22 (*Kirchenpostille*). There are many reasonable arguments for this dating.

33. See also *Luthers storhet,* pp. 18 f., 25–29.

34. *Luthers lära om staten* I, p. 75 (italics mine). Cf. *ibid.*, p. 105.

35. See Henrik Ivarsson, *Predikans uppgift* (Lund, 1956), pp. 19–35, 167–87.

36. Einar Billing, *De heligas gemenskap* (2nd ed.; Uppsala, 1919) pp. 3, 11.

37. *Ibid.*, pp. 14–16.

38. *Ibid.*, p. 17.

39. See *Den svenska folkkyrkan,* pp. 16 f., on the parish pastor's prayer for his congregation, and especially pp. 24 f., where the pastor's own history "merges with an infinitely greater history." On the bishop's intercession for his diocese see Oscar Krook's article in *Einar Billing in memoriam* (Stockholm, 1940), pp. 228 f.

40. Cf. also *De heligas gemenskap,* pp. 38 f.

41. *Our Calling,* pp. 4 f.

42. *Luthers lära om staten* I, p. 107. On the other hand individual, *social* duties are involved, in this sense "social ethics."

43. *Our Calling,* pp. 4 f.

44. *Försoningen,* p. 47.

45. *De etiska tankarna,* pp. 185, 226 f.

46. This is the fundamental thought in the whole book *Den svenska folkkyrkan.* See especially pp. 9–64. Cf. Oscar Krook, *Uppenbarelsebegreppet* I (Stockholm, 1936), pp. 199–201.

47. See Regin Prenter, "Grundtvigs og Einar Billings syn på folkekirken," *Viborgs stifts årbog* (1949), pp. 128–44 (published 1950).

48. *Ibid.*, p. 143.

49. *Den svenska folkkyrkan,* pp. 109 f., where Billing deals in part with "prevenient grace" and *its* ideal form of organization, namely, the territorial parish, and also in part with "personal faith," which easily can become the free church principle. Grace is the "most exalted," faith is the "next highest." There is an obvious danger in

applying such reasoning to questions of organization. But Billing's thought is much more richly differentiated, and much more coherent, when he speaks outside the sphere of church law.

50. Those who plead for Billing's conception of the church ought periodically to read through such books as *The Communion of Saints, Our Calling,* and *God's Presence.* Something new appears with each reading.

51. *Den svenska folkkyrkan,* p. 142. (The passage appeared originally in the lecture at the Pastoral Conference in 1937.)

52. *Ibid.,* p. 110 (italics mine). (These words were spoken in Billing's long address at the 1929 Diet of the Church, when he pleaded for the right of the individual to withdraw from the national church.)

53. *Försoningen,* p. 47. The Church of Sweden has no visible headquarters. It lacks what every territorial parish has.

54. Einar Billing, *I katekesundervisningens tjänst* (2nd ed.; Stockholm, 1943), p. 143. Cf. *Herdabrev,* pp. 85–87.

55. Cf. Ragnar Ekstrom, *Gudsfolk och folkkyrka* (Stockholm, 1923), pp. 182, 194 f.

56. *Den svenska folkkyrkan,* pp. 53, 55. The New Testament word *ecclesia* would be more appropriate in this context than "church" or "congregation." *Ecclesia* represents both the local and the universal aspects.

57. *Ibid.,* p. 111. Billing interprets Mark 10:14 in a way that is similar to Cullmann's interpretation of that text, even though he does not have Cullmann's liturgical and historical theory about the significance of the verb "hinder." The Pauline passage Billing alludes to is 1 Cor. 7:14. Cf. Oscar Cullmann, *Baptism in the New Testament,* trans. J. K. S. Reid ("Studies in Biblical Theology," No. 1; Naperville, Ill.: Alec R. Allenson, Inc., 1950), pp. 76 ff.

58. *Den svenska folkkyrkan,* pp. 12–14, 23 f., and especially 41–43.

59. *Ibid.,* pp. 10 f., 50–52, 133–38.

60. *Ibid.,* p. 53. See also again the remarkable passage (*ibid.,* pp. 41–43) where these two, the church building and the forgiveness of sins, grow together into one.

61. *Ibid.,* p. 50.

62. *Ibid.,* pp. 16, 62, 77. The tendency toward democracy in the official church law begins during the 1950's and 1960's, partly as a result of the general acceptance of Billing's conception of the church.

63. See in this case Björn Kjellin, *Lagen om religionsfrihet* (Stockholm, 1951), pp. 7–24, especially on Billing, pp. 12 f.; in addition see Arne Palmqvist, *De aktuella kyrkobegreppen i Sverige* (Stockholm, 1964), pp. 127–29.

64. *Den svenska folkkyrkan,* p. 123. The statement comes from his speech at the 1929 Diet of the Church, in which he developed a

caricature of the national church as a cultural institution (*ibid.*, p. 124)—a caricature which later, especially during the 1960's, threatened again and again to become a reality. Even in this respect Billing's keen insight was prophetic.

65. *Ibid.*, p. 121 (speech at the 1929 Diet of the Church).

66. See especially *Our Calling*, pp. 39 f.; also *De heligas gemenskap*, pp. 3, 11; also *Den svenska folkkyrkan*, p. 24.

67. Cf. *Luthers lära om staten* I, p. 199.

68. This opinion was not new when Billing expressed it at the 1929 Diet of the Church. It is suggested in *Herdabrev* (1920) and in the article, "Lokalförsamlingen," which he inserted in *Den svenska folkkyrkan* (1930). Cf. *Herdabrev*, pp. 82 f., and *Den svenska folkkyrkan*, p. 55.

69. See the peroration of Billing's speech to the Diet of 1929, *Den svenska folkkyrkan*, pp. 125–27. Cf. *ibid.*, pp. 172–74 (Lecture at the Pastoral Conference in 1937).

70. Luther continued this organizational plan as inherited from the Middle Ages with certain modifications (see *ibid.*, pp. 111–13).

71. The opposition in the *Church* was much stronger than we imagine today. The motion, it was said, "came thirty years too soon." (*Ibid.*, p. 122).

72. As an example one could mention Dietrich von Oppen, "The Era of the Personal," *Man in Community*, ed. Egbert de Vries (New York: Association Press, 1966), pp. 155 ff., especially p. 165. Many other examples could be mentioned.

73. The literary device in Billing's fundamental article (1911) was that the *house* preaches to the pastor. (*Den svenska folkkyrkan*, pp. 40–43.)

74. *Ibid.*, pp. 41 f. (italics mine); cf. p. 43.

75. *De heligas gemenskap*, p. 15; also *Den svenska folkkyrkan*, p. 27.

76. *Försoningen*, p. 47; *Den svenska folkkyrkan*, pp. 40, 43.

77. In spite of Prenter's criticism it is possible to maintain that Billing's idea is largely in agreement with Luther. It is also in conformity with the general Lutheran statement that the church order, "the codes," is free, changeable, flexible. Cf. *Den svenska folkkyrkan*, p. 25; also *Herdabrev*, p. 83; and especially *I katekesundervisningens tjänst*, pp. 140–42.

# CHAPTER V

# UNRESOLVED TENSIONS

Contributions to Billing's literary production came from two sources: the biblical texts and the Reformation (including certain elements in older Swedish Lutheranism). He incorporated both of these into a quite modern frame of reference in which the historical view of the Bible and psychologizing observations were prominent ingredients. Both of these contributions were transformed through this process of incorporation. Billing himself was convinced that by this process the essential content of both was preserved intact and transmitted to the people of the twentieth century. On both of these lines, the interpretation of the Bible and of Luther, the *individual* played a very important role. The whole biblical content, from the Exodus in the Old Testament to the apostolic message proclaimed, according to the New Testament, around the Mediterranean, flowed together into one central point: the forgiveness of sins to the individual. This is the word which the church bears forth from nation to nation. The external organization of the church as it develops manifests visibly that the gospel is for all. But even Billing's arguments in favor of the individual's right to withdrawal from the organization derived principally from his concern about the purity of the *gospel*. The *activity* which sustains the church, and which the church with all its energy has to promote, must not be tarnished by coercion—consequently, free withdrawal.[1]

The tension between the contribution from Israel and the contribution from Luther can be brought together in one formula. The Israel of the Old Testament was at once both church and state. It was both a worshiping congregation and a people like other peoples, with governing laws. The whole civil law was church law. The New Testament congregations, in turn, lacked all possibilities of influencing what was *then* the state: the imperial power of Rome in the Mediterranean world. The Bible in both the Testaments has therefore no developed teaching about the state in the sense of an institution separated from the church. God governs both, but he governs the state with means entirely different from those used in governing the church. He governs the state, and those who believe in God participate actively in this government. Such an elaborate division between God's activity and the activity of those who believe in God cannot be found in the Bible, but Luther made this division. In a sense it also operates in the present, thanks to the democratic practice which makes the members of even the smallest free church responsible for and either positive or negative participants in the activities of the state.[2] The formula in which one can express this tension between the biblical and the Lutheran in Billing's work is connected with these historical matters. Luther operated with two "realms" or "governments," of which the gospel ruled only one, the church. This division had its influence on Billing when he spoke of the organization of the national or territorial parishes. In that context he tended to speak of a grace which was pure, without any kind of demand. In contrast, when he spoke in a pastoral or meditative style *to the individual,* he was much less bound by this division. Then Billing held gift and demand, mercy and righteousness, together in a way that was traditional both in the old Israel and in the Gospels.

Before we define in greater detail the tension in Billing between the biblical and the Lutheran elements, we ought perhaps to emphasize the harmony between them. There is a harmony between them even in respect to some of Billing's somewhat dubious interpretations. As far as Billing was concerned, the Bible began with Exodus. The texts in Genesis and elsewhere dealing with creation were, in principle, insignificant. The historical view determined both creation and the law. When these latter began to appear independently, the age of Judaism had arrived.[3] But in Luther's own thinking both the creation and the law had independent parts to play. No one, however, can describe these independent functions unless he first produces an analysis of the *two kingdoms,* the heavenly and the earthly. As we have seen, Billing tended to make the two into one, the kingdom in which the forgiveness of sins operated as the sole governing principle. Since this tendency clearly influenced Billing's interpretation of Luther, it became much more serious when arguments about the practical question of the organization of the Swedish national church (over against the free churches) came to depend on merely verbal agreements with what Luther had said about the spiritual government, or *ecclesia,* in the context of the sixteenth century. This tendency toward making grace pure and without demand, "cheap grace," thus received additional impetus. Luther, however, incorporated an essential part of the demand into another context, namely, the secular government, the other realm.[4] But if the two realms are reduced to *one,* and if in addition one speaks incessantly in book after book *exclusively about the church,* the biblical and prophetic unity of gift and demand falls apart. Then we create a type of organization which rests on grace apart from any demands—"cheap grace."

The dissolution of the unity between gift and demand became more severe when the doctrine of creation fell by the way. However, it clarifies matters if in analyzing Billing's theology we distinguish between problems he dealt with and problems which he bypassed. The doctrine of creation belongs to the latter. It is one of the lacunae.[5] It is significant to analyze even such blank spaces and the unexpressed presuppositions behind these silent assumptions. In the following parts we will discuss this series of neglected problems. The absence of these elements in Billing's work derived from his failure to develop a definitive anthropology and from his neglect of the relationship between theology and philosophy (see Chap. VII below). But there are other questions about which Billing has spoken, albeit differently in different contexts. The problem of the unity between *gift* and *demand* belongs here. The differences in his statements about this matter depended on his two sources, Israel and Luther. It is the tension between these two which we must analyze in this present chapter.

Without any doubt the contribution from Israel, his biblical theology, was the most *productive* element in Billing's literary work. One can also incorporate the Reformation element into this biblical theology. Even the expressions borrowed from Luther about the forgiveness of sins as a gift offered through the external church organization can be interpreted in the light of the biblical historical conception and can be understood as a form of exodus offered to the individual.[6] Above all, however, one can incorporate the doctrine of creation into Billing's interpretation of the exodus. The territorial parish, too, with its "fences" and "ditches" saturated with grace, is a combination of creation and salvation.[7] But this gospel which seeks everyone in the parish can also be interpreted as a vertical "word" from above, as it is in modern Christomonism. Exodus, on the other hand, includes God's rule even over those who do not believe, God's sovereignty over Pharaoh and the Persian king. This is a direct work of God in the world, and it is and remains the essential center of the doctrine of creation.[8] The exodus which God gives to the individual through the death and resurrection of Christ is not different from God's saving acts in the old Israel. God's sovereignty over the world becomes even more strongly accentuated by the active, yet quite helpless, part which the Roman imperial power had to play: the enrollment in Bethlehem, the crucifixion on Golgotha, the suffering of martyrdom within the empire. His biblical theology is the richest heritage that Billing has given us.

This heritage provides abundant material for the field of *ethics.* Everywhere the threads run together into ethics, both social and individual. God's "righteous acts" toward the small and unjustly oppressed people of Israel involved immediate consequences in regard to their legal system. The law always conceived of the stranger, the orphan, and the widow as living in the same perilous circumstances as Israel in Egypt, where he who had power was free to do whatever he desired.[9] Yahweh continued his work as the righteous and merciful judge as he watched over the unfortunates in the hostile environment. For the same purpose he sent prophets to the people, and they continually reiterated the same refrain: cruelty toward the poor must be stigmatized as evil wherever it appears.[10] It is not difficult to draw the line from this prophetic attitude toward social problems in Israel to consequences for the relationship of the church to the needs of modern society. That line was drawn even more easily at a time when the workingman's struggle for justice was just beginning. Billing did in fact draw that line, briefly in *Our Calling (Vår kallelse),* more fully in his lectures on "The Ethical Problems in the Modern Labor Movement" ("De etiska problemen i den moderna arbetarfrågan").

But he drew that line even more clearly from the New Testament exodus for the individual, and from the forgiveness of sins as free gift to the individual, straight to the ethical implications for this individual's intercourse with his fellowmen. This line flashes forth in Jesus' parable of the unmerciful servant (Matt. 18:23–35), and again in the one petition in the Our Father where forgiveness is mentioned, the only petition in the prayer that includes a moment of ethical self-examination. We could say that this was the principal line in Billing's ethics.[11] In this context his facility for variations and his

brilliant ethical insight appeared at their best. It is quite natural, therefore, that personally he had a much more stimulating effect on his contemporaries than he achieved through
his books. Individual ethics can never be fully expressed in
words. It must be exemplified again and again in actions and
fellowship.

It is unfortunate, therefore, that Billing did not give to the
great number of concrete statements found in the letters of
Paul concerning the individual Christian's course of action in
following Christ the same thorough attention that he gave to
the ethical materials in the Old Testament and in the Gospels.
It is unfortunate because these Pauline texts consistently contain admonitions about the ethical implications of *baptism*.
They are in a sense texts about the *church*, about the body
that follows the Head through death to resurrection. It is
sometimes said, in a stereotyped fashion, that Billing never
discovered the New Testament conception of the church, and
that he therefore let the New Testament be concerned solely
with the individual. When we consider the results of the col-
lectivistic ethical ideas which the exegetical renaissance has
produced in its study of the church, it would seem quite doubt-
ful that Billing is the one who is lagging behind. From an
exegetical point of view his emphasis on the individual was
rather his strong point. We can say this quite confidently in
view of the fact that we need a new and constructive effort to
define the role of the church in community life today. In this
area it is impossible to ignore the individuals and their neigh-
borly relationships, which are different for every person
involved.

But Billing could have achieved something positive, something *in line with his great work in biblical theology,* if he had
pointed out the unity of righteousness and mercy, judgment
and grace, gift and demand, in the ethos of the congregations
as they appear in the New Testament letters.[12] In that case

baptism might have become much more significant in his works than it actually is. His thought about the national church made use only of infant baptism as an expression of prevenient grace. This exclusive emphasis threatened to make baptism a quietistic part of a church organization, the territorial parish, that lacked the element of demand and commitment. The demand and commitment inherent in baptism were kept alive in the Swedish situation by another type of organization, the free churches. But these churches could do this only by an equally tragic one-sidedness in the other direction.

The free church type of organization in Billing's time had lost another elementary feature of the New Testament: the thought that God is the subject of the action in baptism, and that he actually *does* something in reference to the one baptized. The older Baptist groups, which have exercised a strong influence on almost all the European free churches, regarded baptism as man's own act of confession. Under the influence of New Testament exegesis these free churches are now in the process of correcting this one-sided conception. This tendency certainly affects present-day Baptist communions.[13] At the same time, due not least to Billing's bold motion about free withdrawal, the territorial parishes in the Swedish national church are in the process of a restructuring that must make them more conscious of baptismal responsibility. Here a possibility dawns for carrying the heritage from Billing further *in faithfulness to his work in biblical theology*. Such an extension would not dissolve Billing's theology, it would simply develop its implications in a new situation for which Billing himself to a large extent supplied the impetus. Since the idea of demand and responsibility in baptism is coming alive in the national church, and since the idea of gift in baptism is similarly becoming appreciated among the free churches, the New Testament may in the long run bring forth ecumenical results which will affect even the pattern of organization. I would maintain that to work further in this direction is more in line with Billing's theological effort than to repeat mechanically his statements about the organization of the national church as the expression of "the forgiveness of sins to the people of Sweden."

What Billing had to say about forms of organization was only a small part of the abundant material, oral and written, which came almost like a flood whenever he touched on the theme of the forgiveness of sins. Furthermore, many of these statements simply repeated verbatim what Luther had said about "the spiritual government." The territorial parishes are made up of *individuals,* each of whom has his own workaday world and his own history. When Billing spoke to these individuals, his words acquired that remarkable and illuminating power which time and two World Wars have not been able to diminish. In that context his thoughts poured forth "like the rays of the sun from *one* glowing core, namely, the gospel of the forgiveness of sins."[14] We should not imagine that we conform to Billing's conception of the national church if we cannot interpret the forgiveness of sins in this personal form to the individuals of our day. Our agreement with him cannot be simply a repetition—on the level of legislation, or in conferences with the ministries of ecclesiastical affairs—of his arguments in dealing with the questions of church law common to the 1920's. The spiritual legacy of a significant personality cannot be institutionalized without becoming impoverished and finally lost.

In his historical description of Jesus' work as reported in the Gospels, Billing sought in a sense to express something of the energy with which he himself sought to reach the *individual* man. If it is really the gospel that is involved, the work cannot assume any other form. In spite of the immense scope of the undertaking, the ministry must be characterized by patience and serenity, reaching one person at a time without

hurrying.[15] The work that the Father had given Jesus to do
for the individual had to be carried on at this tempo.

Jesus' purposive action looked toward a thoroughgoing reformation of Israel's social life. His work involved a new aeon, a universal rebirth of the whole cosmic order (Mark 10:30; Matt.
19:28). He proclaimed *this* kingdom of God as imminently near,
and he gave man the right to expect that this kingdom would come
through his own word and work. And yet he confined his work to
seeking and assembling a few individual persons. How great the
distance between what was expected and what was and could be
accomplished by that kind of ministry was revealed best by a word
of Jesus himself: "Fear not, little flock, for it is your Father's
good pleasure to give you the kingdom" (Luke 12:32). Between
"the little flock" and "the kingdom of God" the distance was
as great as between heaven and earth. As this word indicates, it
cannot even be said that the one is the beginning of the other.
That Jesus confined his work to reaching individuals was the
main reason why not only the masses but also John and his disciples found it difficult to recognize in him the one who was to
come. . . . Such a conception of a "messianic" ministry could not
be found either in the old national expectation or in later apocalyptic expectations. He continued on this course in spite of the
fact that this conduct of his work aroused disappointment and
impatience. He did not hesitate for a moment, because the revelation he had received convinced him that this was the Father's
will for his life.[16]

For Billing the church meant that Jesus continued "to go
from nation to nation," carrying on the same ministry to the
individual as he had done in Israel. As a bishop Billing confined his ministry to one diocese, Västerås, and assumed
responsibility for its territorial parishes. The ultimate purpose
of his ministry was to bring the forgiveness of sins to *individuals*. Such a ministry is generally secret and unobserved.
One cannot discover it by enumerating episcopal "measures."
In Billing's case, however, there are good reasons for including
among the results of his theological contribution something of
what he did as bishop. In a sense even his work as bishop was
a continuation of his literary production as professor.

NOTES TO CHAPTER V

1. See especially Einar Billing, *Den svenska folkkyrkan* (2nd ed.; Stockholm, 1963), p. 121.

2. In contrast, modern Christian interpretations of life devote little *reflection* to this division. All Christians, therefore, who do not today seek to abolish the police system accept, often without reflection, positive violence in some form.

3. See Einar Billing, *De etiska tankarna i urkristendomen* (2nd ed. enlarged; Stockholm, 1921), pp. 282–85; cf. pp. 380 f.

4. Cf. Einar Billing, *Luthers lära om staten* I (Uppsala, 1900) pp. 86–89; cf. also his *Our Calling,* rev. trans. Conrad Bergendoff ("Facet Books – Social Ethics Series," 1; Philadelphia: Fortress Press, 1964), p. 18.

5. That the first chapters in Genesis are Luther's chief texts (see *Luthers lära om staten* I, p. 124), but are not significant for Billing, and that the list of biblical references in *Försoningen* ([2nd ed.; Stockholm, 1921], p. 145) includes none from Genesis but begins with Exodus, indicate clearly Billing's attitude. Cf. also Einar Billing, *I katekesundervisningens tjänst* (2nd ed.; Stockholm, 1943), pp. 41, 213 (to n. 8).

6. Cf. Gösta Wrede, *Kyrkosynen i Einar Billings teologi* (Stockholm, 1966), pp. 158 f. (references also to unpublished materials), and the conclusions drawn on p. 190.

7. *Den svenska folkkyrkan,* p. 34, where "faith in creation" stands expressed side by side with "faith in forgiveness."

8. Cf. *De etiska tankarna,* pp. 93, 183; *Försoningen,* pp. 23 f.

9. Cf. *De etiska tankarna,* p. 128.

10. *Ibid.,* p. 101.

11. *Ibid.,* pp. 369 f. It would not be an exaggeration to insist that *all* of Billing's shorter works are of this character.

12. The claim cannot be made that *Försoningen,* pp. 62–68, provides an analysis of this ethos of the congregation. There are suggestions, but that is all. Unfortunately the manuscript of Part II of *De etiska tankarna* is in such a form that it cannot readily be used. But the important point is that these manuscripts have not *influenced* other people, at least not to the same extent as his far-reaching teaching about infant baptism. With this teaching Billing has already contributed a chapter to the history of the church in Sweden.

13. In our Swedish context we may note the Baptist contributions in the book *Samfund i självprövning* (Stockholm, 1964), pp. 85–101.

14. *Our Calling,* p. 4. The words refer to Luther's thoughts, but the presentation as a whole indicates that they apply also to Billing himself.

15. *De etiska tankarna,* pp. 351 f., 388–95.

16. *Ibid.,* pp. 391 f.

# Chapter VI

# THE BISHOP
# AND HIS INFLUENCE

## 1. Einar Billing as Bishop After 1920

We have already stated that Billing produced nothing basically new after 1920. In September of that year, at the time of his consecration as bishop, he published his *Pastoral Letter (Herdabrev)*, which could be said to represent a compendium of his previous work and also the capstone of his theological edifice. The bishop's office provided him with a position in which he could be active without writing books. What he did as bishop was really to follow out the implications of this theological point of view. We have already touched on most of this work as we have tried to give an account of his theology up to the end of his tenure as professor. Among these we may again enumerate his proposal of 1929 for free withdrawal from the church, his review of the development of the conception of the national *(folk)* church in his lecture at the Pastoral Conference of 1937, and the review of the relationship of Sweden to evangelical Christianity, a guest lecture delivered at the University of Königsberg in 1927.[1] We may add a couple of other details, also previously mentioned: his assistance in the formulation of the 1922 letter to Lambeth in regard to intercommunion with the Anglicans and his proposal at the ecumenical meeting in Stockholm in 1925 for a study center in Geneva. Most important, however, is his hymn, Number 380 in the *Swedish Psalmbook* of 1937, written in 1922 after he had returned to the city where he had spent his youth.

If we regard the impact of Billing's work after 1920 as chiefly the result of his strength as a person, I believe that his influence as *preacher* and *speaker* surpassed everything else. This aspect of his work is naturally difficult to assess after so many years have passed. After he was consecrated bishop, he confined his preaching and speaking to his own diocese. This, too, is characteristic of his faithfulness to his calling. For him personally, preaching was a very severe and difficult task.[2] His agony can only partially be explained on the basis of his nervous temperament. The real cause was his own theological conception of "the word." When he entered the pulpit, he carried the responsibility of handling God's means of grace, which implied life or death for those who came to listen. Unfortunately, very few of his sermons and public addresses delivered in his diocese have been preserved. The contents of his posthumous book *God's Presence (Guds närhet)* stem mostly from the period before 1920. Evidently there were more people in Uppsala who were willing and able to take notes than there were in the diocese of Västerås, from 1920 to 1939.

When we consider Billing's influence during his years as bishop we must also take note of the development known as "the young church movement" *(ungkyrkorörelsen)*. After "motif research" began to dominate systematic theology at Lund, and when, a few years later, the exegetical department in Uppsala completely abandoned the problems which had occupied Billing, this young church movement came quickly to be regarded as an event of the past. But that which at a certain time is passé in Uppsala and Lund may just at that moment be most flourishing out in the field. This truth applies to the young church movement. It is true that J. A. Eklund

and Einar Billing were the first representatives of this movement among the Swedish bishops, and that both of them had
left their bishoprics by 1938 and 1939. Nevertheless, around
the midpoint of the century these newer theological currents
had not had a chance to consolidate their positions in the
leadership of the church before the arrival of the crisis in
connection with the decision to admit women to the ordained
ministry. When this decision was made, leadership came from
the heirs of the young church movement. Manfred Björkquist
and Olle Nystedt functioned in a remarkable way in building
bridges between the earliest period of the movement (about
1908–10) and the period of consolidation during the 1960's.[3]
Billing's *Pastoral Letter* came out in a new edition in 1962,
forty years after its first publication. The collection of essays,
*The Swedish National Church (Den svenska folkkyrkan)*, was
published again in 1963 with additional material, some of
which was written before World War I. These publications
indicate clearly a late young church renaissance in the Swedish
church. From a *theological* point of view they signify a revival
of Einar Billing's theology. In the area of theological scholarship he was beyond question the most prominent leader in the
movement.[4]

It is obvious that this development presents great problems
for the congregational and theological situation in Sweden.
Billing's theology, which has proved to be so unusually effective in the practical life of the church, has now practically no
representative among members of the theological faculties.
Theological work in Uppsala and Lund proceeds now on an
entirely different wavelength, since the significance of the
biblical word as proclaimed in the present world is seldom an
object of discussion. But many of Billing's terms have become
titles of respect. They are attached now to everyone who is
in favor of the ordination of women, no matter how ignorant
of Billing's writings he may be, or how flaccid and publicity-

hungry he may appear. One does not call oneself *"young-churchly"* anymore, that sounds too romantic, but *"national (folk) churchman"* is a very much beloved designation, especially in the Swedish daily press. The term "national church" has lost practically all its definitive meaning. An investigation would very likely show, unfortunately, that this term is used most often to describe an organization in which the people in one way or another have the power of decision. It is now relatively seldom used to describe a church which *seeks to reach* the people with the gospel. In other words, Billing's term is used in a sense which Billing explicitly rejected.[5] This situation involves serious problems in regard to the Billing legacy. Sometimes a theologian derives more joy from opposition than from applause.

In this situation it is appropriate to emphasize strongly one characteristic feature in Billing's conception of the church: his constant and sometimes one-sided accentuation of the independence of the church over against the state. As early as 1900, in his *Luther's Teaching Concerning the State (Luthers lära om staten),* he spoke depreciatingly of the secular government as being of lower rank than the spiritual realm.[6] His attitude in this respect was typical of him, but it is questionable that it represented the view of the sixteenth century. In all his references to events in Swedish church history Billing invariably selected situations in which the leaders of the church maintained the freedom of the gospel over against a power-hungry and despotic state. As examples we may mention Olaus Petri's independent attitude toward Gustavus Vasa, Laurentius Petri's struggle against John III, the bold defiance of Prince Carl and King Sigismund by the members of the Diet of Uppsala (1593), and the stalwart opposition of Johannes Rudbeckius to the plans of Gustavus Adolphus for centralizing the government of the church under the state.[7] Nothing was too trivial to be ignored in this great array of protests. He mentioned with approval even the Diets of the Church in 1893 (the question of the confessions) and in 1925 (the law regarding burial), because these involved at least a rejection of directives from the crown.[8] Sometimes Billing appeared to run the risk of seeming to be a person with an inferiority complex who had to "compensate" by using powerful and exaggerated words. We find an example of this in the closing words of his address to the 1929 Diet of the Church, when he asserted: "We in our church have no fear whatever for the future." He then added:

> We are absolutely certain that we cannot be harmed by any power in this land, if we but seriously and sincerely devote ourselves to our religious task. *We are stronger than every other power, and stronger than all powers banded together.*[9]

But this was a frequently recurring theme in his thinking. Whenever Billing spoke of or to the state, he spoke with unmistakable self-assurance. The source of this self-assurance was the gospel. The foundation of the state might be destroyed, but *he* represented an eternal kingdom.

In this connection the important point is that *Billing's criticism of the Swedish government increased during his years as bishop.* He had never before painted such a dark picture of the conditions of the Swedish national church as he did in his lecture at the 1937 Pastoral Conference in his diocese. The specific issues which troubled him were the law compelling pastors to officiate, even against their conscience, at all weddings; the superficiality of the confirmation practice; the lack of initiative on the part of the Diet of the Church; etc. Those who today like to pose as being interested in "the national church" have not paid any special attention to these points.[10]

If the heritage from Billing is to be preserved, we in Sweden need to turn our attention to some concealed problems within the church, problems which very likely cannot be resolved without friction with the state. If we permit the independence of the church in its relation to the state to be safeguarded by the opponents of the national church, it will be these opponents who at an important point fulfill Billing's intentions. But in that case the "fulfillment" will very likely not be based on the gospel. Then there is danger that it will be the New Testament "commandments" that will govern the church.

### 2. Billing's Later Influence in Sweden

We now leave our consideration of Billing, the young church movement, and the idea of the national church in order to investigate the aftereffects of Billing's theology in Sweden. Our analysis will be concerned with three specific issues which stand outside of Billing's own writings, although we do not propose to present a complete account of these issues. Subsequent to Billing's pioneering work, many factors affected Swedish Luther research as well as Lundensian motif research. The "high church" tendency, too, is a multi-faceted phenomenon. And the relationship between the national church and the free churches presents a varied picture of opposites and connections in inner tension with one another. It is easy to define the selective principle operating in our immediate considerations, in which we make three subdivisions. Our only purpose is to point out such material within each of these subdivisions as reveals the influence of Billing's work. The effect of Billing's theology is not confined to potential disciples or to persons who themselves quote Billing as authority.

*a. Luther Research and Lundensian Theology*

On Sunday, September 19, 1920, Einar Billing was consecrated Bishop of the Diocese of Västerås in Uppsala Cathedral. On Friday, May 21, 1921, Anders Nygren defended his doctoral dissertation before the faculty at the University of Lund. These events in Uppsala and Lund took place during the same academic year, and they are a very definite line of demarcation in the more recent history of Swedish theology.

There were no direct connections between Billing and Nygren, at least not in the initial situation.[11] But between them stands Gustaf Aulén, who studied under Billing at Uppsala and was in close contact with him up until 1913. Aulén was Nygren's professor at Lund and later on, from 1924 to 1933, his colleague in the theological faculty. If one asks who among the *university* theologians has perpetuated Billing's general attitude and methodology as researcher and thinker, the answer must be one man, Gustaf Aulén.[12] Billing's successors at Uppsala have not preserved Billing's contribution to theology with anything of the same energy as Aulén. This means that it is primarily through the study of systematic theology at *Lund* that Billing's influence remains. This surprising situation needs to be further clarified.

The single example of a scholarly work in Sweden which is strongly influenced by Billing's methodology is, in my opinion, Arvid Runestam's first book, *Christian Liberty in Luther and Melanchthon (Den kristliga friheten hos Luther och Melanchthon),* published in 1917. This genuinely impressive book has been too generally ignored in later Swedish studies of Luther's theology. But the influence of Billing disappeared very quickly in Runestam's later works. There are traces of it in the little book, *The Freedom of the Will (Viljans frihet),* published in 1921, but in Runestam's production during his time as professor these traces became less and less noticeable. Instead, Runestam became interested in Freud, Marx, Scheler, and Künkel. Sometimes there appears a kind of revolt against Billing, as in *Love, Faith, and Imitation (Kärlek, tro, efterföljd),* published in 1931.[13] Torsten Bohlin, who for some time studied under Billing, and Sigfrid von Engeström, who was a personal friend of Billing, have never followed Billing's typical methodology. Runestam, Bohlin, and Von Engeström have kept Billing's name prominent at Uppsala, but no literary productions along Billing's line of thought have been produced there. This situation prevails even today.

Gustaf Aulén, who has been connected with Lund since 1913, has had an entirely different outlook during his entire literary career from before World War I to the 1960's. Four of Billing's unique principles of theological work determine Aulén's theological stance: (1) The doctrine of *the atonement* in which God is the acting subject stands in the center. (2) *The conception of the church* with God as acting subject in the means of grace comes directly from the word of the atonement. (3) *The Bible and Luther* are the two great sources between which the theologian alternates in his work. (4) Lastly, but perhaps most characteristically, *Luther is the biblical interpreter for the whole church.* Luther is *doctor ecclesiae universalis,* not "Lutheran," not the entrance figure into Lutheran orthodoxy. Aulén carefully maintains the difference between Luther and later Lutheranism.

These four points, which were typical of Einar Billing and of Gustaf Aulén, recur also in the works of Anders Nygren, Ragnar Bring, Per Erik Persson, and myself. They may appear in various terminology and forms, but until now they have been present in almost all Lundensian studies in systematic theology. Many foreigners who read Swedish theological literature today regard these features as specifically Lundensian, but we must admit here that all four of these features come from Uppsala via Aulén. It is most important to note that none of these four features can be found in clear and radical form in any Swedish theologian's work before Einar Billing. With the assistance of Nathan Söderblom at some points, Billing combined these four features and created this fundamentally clear theological structure.[14]

Here we must insert two marginal notes. In the first place, Einar Billing's theology contained a number of ideas which have *not* been continued in Lund. In the second place, other elements, *new* ideas, have appeared in Lund, especially through the works of Anders Nygren. These new elements were foreign to Billing, and their acceptance, especially in respect to methodology, resulted in dissolving some of his central points. It will clarify matters if we discuss these two marginal notes separately.

In the first place, what has been lost? The loss of the anchorage in the Old Testament was a great misfortune. Gradually the biblical material became less and less extensive, until it became impossible to discover any independent content in the Old Testament part of the Bible. Motif research promoted this development. At the same time Billing's characteristic emphasis on the *individual* disappeared from the exegesis of the New Testament. The individual became enclosed in the church and its *koinonia*. Both of these losses contributed to a certain softness in Lundensian theology toward the high church tendency that since 1940 has appeared in Sweden.[15]

Now, what has been added? The new elements came essentially from one man, Anders Nygren. Since the year 1921 he has slowly and methodically constructed his own systematic program, which has for a long time characterized Lund. It has also restricted the elements coming from Billing via Aulén in the Lundensian theology. Through Nygren's influence Aulén himself changed, and so did Bring.[16] The most important new elements are (1) the establishment of a philosophical basis, which Nygren worked out, especially in the period 1921–23, and (2) motif research, which he defined precisely in his works in the history of ideas, 1930–36. In this context systematic theology became in principle identified with the history of ideas. But as a result it became impossible to ask Billing's *fundamental question* about the significance of the biblical word in relation to the man *now* living in the present.

It is true that since 1940 no one in Lund or anywhere else has conducted motif research according to the program set up by Nygren. But the negative effect remains, and the fear of a "kerygmatic" stance lingers on among most working theologians. The result is that from a methodological point of view Billing belongs to the past.[17]

It is possible, however, to exaggerate the divisive effect of the struggle relative to methodology. *No* theological methodology rejects, for example, an immanent investigation of great and comprehensive systems from the past. Systematic theologians with quite disparate points of view are able to meet, as they seek to understand a difficult body of material from within. Luther research in Sweden has become such a meeting place with open possibilities of conversation among all those who know what is contained in the many volumes of the Weimar Edition. Einar Billing was the first of the many modern Swedish students in this field. He started with his doctoral dissertation of 1900, although at that time his work had to be based mostly on the old Erlangen Edition of Luther's works. His position as a pioneer brings him even today into contact with those young students who are beginning their work in Reformation history. During the 1920's the dominant interest of Swedish studies in Luther was in the field of soteriology and justification. The area of Luther's teaching about the state received relatively little attention. The change came in 1934 with Herbert Olsson's pioneering work, *The Fundamental Problem in Luther's Social Ethics (Grundproblemet i Luthers socialetik)*. Since that time the question of Luther's view of "the world," or "the earth," has become the subject of several studies. Gustaf Törnvall's doctoral thesis of 1940 on Luther's teaching concerning the two realms was directly connected with Billing's work of 1900, and could hardly have been written without that pioneering study.[18] This book was quickly translated into German and had marked effect even outside of Sweden. What I myself have had to say about Luther's doctrine of the call belongs in this context. In that discussion I naturally paid considerable attention to Billing and his attempt to reduce "the two realms" to one. Luther research is perhaps the area in which Billing continues to be most influential, and this is, paradoxically enough, the area in which his contribution is most questionable.[19]

### b. *The High Church Tendency*

Einar Billing really did not come into contact with any high church tendency other than the Anglican. There is considerable evidence that he shared his father's somewhat nonchalant opinion about such movements: they were "childish absurdities."[20] But since Billing's death in 1939 more serious forms of high church piety have arisen in Sweden.

If we were to mention one area of *teaching* that could be called high church, it would have to be the doctrine of the ministry: the thesis that a certain external form, "the historical episcopate," is essential and necessary in the church. In actual practice, however, this doctrine often is expressed in an interest in worship, in prayer, and in the sacraments. Consecrations of bishops occur rather infrequently, but the Sunday morning service comes every week and the canonical hours daily. In a country where the worship service is often performed routinely, and where theology neglects the function of the means of grace *now,* in the present, a certain malaise often manifests itself in a swift growth of high church tendencies. This was the situation in Sweden from about 1935 to 1960. When theology becomes history, the high church tendency begins to flourish quite naturally. The reason for this is that in such a situation the high church group is the only one that speaks theologically and emphatically about the worship which *now* takes place. Among the increasing number of adherents to this point of view, usually young people, only a very few have any clear understanding of a special doctrine of the ministry. These

few are usually concerned with the doctrine of apostolic succession as a guarantee of the validity of the Sacrament of the
Lord's Supper. The rest have joined the crowd as a result of
the common spiritual malaise in the country. Nobody has
spoken to them about the significance of worship in the present—nobody, that is, but the high church people.

If for the moment we forget about the specific doctrine of
the ministry, we have to note that the general interest in
worship as a present act derives from the Reformation. *Con-
fessio Augustana* (the Augsburg Confession), which has no
article about the inspiration of the Bible, has placed its teaching about the word in an article on the office of preaching.
This Lutheran procedure is so strange that it strikes an out-
sider as surprising.[21] "The office of preaching" in this context
means simply a man's mouth being utilized *now* by the word
of the gospel, *viva vox*. Both Luther and the Lutheran confessions rejected all hierarchical theories (see, for example,
the Smalcald Articles). What was affirmed was the service of
*worship*. The thesis that the Sunday morning service is the
natural place for weekly communion is not specifically high
church. On the contrary, this statement is made repeatedly in
the Lutheran Reformation, both in Germany by Luther
himself and in Sweden by the Swedish reformers. That in
twentieth century Sweden this thesis should need to be defended as something new, and in addition should need the
support of groups influenced by Anglicanism, cannot be characterized as anything but a symptom of decay in the current
Lutheranism of the country.

We must further point out that Billing's theology as a whole
is an interpretation of worship. It is the interpretation of infant
baptism, of the preaching of the gospel, of everything that the
parish church with its baptismal font, its pulpit, and its altar
represents. From one point of view the young church movement was entirely a rediscovery of common worship in the

parish church, which at that time was looked upon rather contemptuously.[22] But on the other hand it completely failed to
find a place for the Lord's Supper as the center of worship.[23]
In this area the high church movement caused a positive
change from 1930 onward. One man who was a pioneer in
this area was Yngve Brilioth[24] with his book, *Eucharistic Faith
and Practice (Nattvarden i evangeliskt gudstjänstliv)*, first published in 1926. The most remarkable feature of Brilioth's
work was that he used the categories of worship. He had no
dogmatic theory about the office of bishop, and he had no
exegetical theory about the origin of episcopal succession in
early Christianity. When the high church tendency entered its
dogmatic period, and then later, due to influences from
Uppsala, its exegetical period, Brilioth vehemently rejected
these new theories. The Swedish high church adherents,
in their struggle to extricate themselves from their present
frustrating entanglement, would receive much help from a
renewed study of Brilioth's works. He was influenced by the
earlier contributions of the Uppsala of Nathan Söderblom and
Einar Billing.

In these earlier works one constantly finds a critical attitude
toward every specific theory about the external form of the
office. Such specific theories about the office of the ministry,
if present at all, are usually an important and critical point
in high churchism. Billing regarded all such theories about
the office as untenable, even on exegetical grounds.[25] If one
approaches Jesus from the point of view of rabbinism, which
is a reasonable and historical approach, the specific feature in
this context is the *absence* of any prescription for church
order. In speaking of the *individual*, Billing writes:

> It would be easy to quote many more words of Jesus which show
> to what extent his whole outlook was determined by his thought
> of the value of the individual. His work as a whole furnishes the
> decisive proof. The examples we have cited can be seen in their

true perspective only when we notice what is *left out.* He instituted
no definite ordinances for the little flock, or "congregation,"
which he had gathered around himself. We can imagine what a
rabbi might have found necessary to prescribe. Matthew 18:15 ff.
could possibly be regarded as an embryonic order for the congregation, but the same process is present here as in Matthew's
compilation of the Sermon on the Mount. A comparison with
Luke is instructive in this instance also (cf. Matt. 18:15 ff. with
Luke 17:3 ff.). If we keep this in mind, we see at once that Jesus
was thinking not about an order for the congregation, but rather
about how human souls who are about to become lost may be
"gained" (Matt. 18:15). Whatever one may think in regard to the
disputed question about Jesus and the sacraments, that conception
is entirely false which imagines that he regarded them from the
point of view of order, ceremonialism, or cult practice. Jesus' task
was to gather and bring *persons* to commitment, and to induct them
into his own personal relationship with the Father. His task was to
ask the Father for and to send out those persons who were to
continue the task of seeking and gathering. *This work* was his
way of establishing the church.[26]

It is well known that Billing's attitude characterized the
answer which the Swedish bishops forwarded to the Anglican
Bishops' Conference in 1922. The Anglican theories about
succession were specifically rejected, but intercommunion was
accepted on a different basis. Both of the churches, Anglican
and Swedish, serve the *gospel,* although using different external orders.[27] The main theological point was entirely the
work of Einar Billing. At the episcopal consecration on September 19, 1920, when Billing and Victor Rundgren were
consecrated, Anglican bishops participated for the first time.
The attempts of the Swedish high church groups to impress
upon the Swedish church a wrong interpretation of the 1922
settlement have failed. They mistakenly assert that episcopal
succession was the real basis of the agreement. Billing's typical
structure of the argument on this point, as on many others,
has become the official position of the Swedish church.

But in spite of this contrast between Billing and high
church tendencies, a contrast which can be localized in the

doctrine of the ministry, we must not forget the inner, positive relationship. Einar Billing was the first one in Sweden whose theology issued in *ecclesiology*; he had no interpretation of creation and law, no "anthropological theology." Furthermore, he was the first one who gave a fundamental significance to the external *form of organization* for the fulfillment of the function of the church in proclaiming the gospel. At this point Regin Prenter's criticism is relevant.[28] It is true indeed that Billing was concerned with the organization of the territorial parish, not with any certain type of ministry. But if the type of organization has already acquired a fundamental significance, it may be easy to fall victim to the supposition that there is something like a New Testament congregational order. It would not really be strange if Billing's own conception of church organization were determined by his polemical opposition to the free church type of organization.

*c. Opposition to the Free Churches*

The description of life in the parish of Hagby and Ramsta that Gerda Billing presented eleven years after her husband's death in her book, *The Unforgettable Parsonage (Den oförglömliga prästgården),* is somewhat surprising. The parish was strongly free-church-oriented. Billing was obviously giving frequent and serious consideration to the free church leaders in the parish, trying to find a *positive* relationship between their activity and the parish church.[29] He evidently found it somewhat difficult to motivate this positive attitude theologically. In his letters to his father in Lund he tried again and again to explain and excuse himself. He also had to be careful because his associate pastor, who was from the western coast of Sweden, where he had been influenced by the conservative Lutheranism associated with Henrik Schartau (d. 1825), was strongly negative in regard to any association with the free church people. This colleague was the vice-pastor during the time Billing was in Uppsala tending to his duties as professor.

It is surprising that Billing actually entertained this *desire* for
a positive relationship with the free church movement.

On this "ecumenical home front" Einar Billing evidently
worked according to a definite pattern.

> I have really more and more come to the conviction that we
> cannot be satisfied with a negative policy. On the contrary, we
> ought *to take these people with us in the work of the church*
> even while we emphasize the fundamental difference. . . . I do
> have several plans, but we will have to proceed slowly. The great-
> est difficulty in my position is that I can spend so little time out
> here in the parish.[30]

The context indicates that Billing consistently tried to establish contact with free church people and that he did so in the
parish where he was chief pastor. This whole program in its
"ineffectiveness" is very significant in regard to Billing's Lutheran conception of the call. But the tentative attempts in
Hagby and Ramsta are sufficient to indicate that his conception of the national church was not in principle anti-ecu-
menical. In the territorial parishes, with their definite boundaries, it is possible to work together with the free church
people, whose conception of the church involves rejection of
the territorial boundaries of the parish.[31]

When the free churches tried to establish their type of
organization on the basis of a New Testament congregational
principle, the passage Matthew 18:15–17 played an important role. Church discipline became the means for the establishment of order in the congregation.[32] When Billing sought
to refute the argument on this point, he did not simply ignore
Matthew's words or try to cite other passages. On the contrary,
he *interpreted* Matthew 18. What this text prescribes is that
no effort is too great when it involves "gaining" a single individual. The part of the text which interprets the whole is found
at the end of verse 15: *"you have gained your brother."* What
follows indicates the efforts which must be resorted to when
the individual himself fails to gain his fellowman. He may

enlist the help of "two or three," and finally the whole congregation may be alerted in order to seek and gain *just one*.
According to Billing the parable of the shepherd who leaves
everything and goes out to find *one* lost sheep is a parallel
to this misinterpreted passage on "church discipline" (Luke
15:4 ff.).[33] Matthew placed the parable of the lost sheep immediately before the so-called church discipline passage, and
in substance the two passages belong together. The following
section, which speaks of the *duty to forgive* (Matt. 18:19–35),
also belongs here. The parallel passage in Luke (17:3 f.)
combines these two elements: the duty to rebuke and the duty
to forgive a brother.[34]

Billing incorporated "the church discipline passage," therefore, into the framework of seeking and forgiving an erring
brother, into the exodus framework. But he also made some
interesting new observations that are of great significance for
the conception of the national church.

> In the first place, it reminds us, more directly perhaps than any
> other word in the New Testament, that the task and function of
> seeking and conquering love includes also "the rebuke." It is
> indispensable that sin should be brought to light and condemned.
> In the second place, it reminds us of the joint responsibility of
> the whole congregation in this matter. If we hold these two ideas
> together, we realize that they who regarded this passage as the
> primary text of "church discipline" were right. . . . We see then
> also that it is fully relevant to our time and fully applicable to
> our church. We see, too, that it has never ceased to operate in
> various forms in the church. But it is absolutely *necessary* that
> *all of us* pitch in and help one another much more seriously than
> hitherto, in order that this principle *may be truly applied*.[35]

It is characteristic of Billing's cavalier treatment of his most
original contributions that he included this exegetical analysis
in the 1922 *Yearbook of the Diocese of Västerås (Julboken
för Västerås stift)*, where it was practically buried. Nor did he
ever follow up these suggestive ideas with concrete examples
of possible "applications." Ecumenicity in Hagby and Ramsta

and church discipline in the diocese are like the flower of which the psalmist says, "its place knows it no more." But in both cases it is the principle involved that is most important. Just as the letters from the small pastorate indicate that the conception of the national church includes cooperation with the free churches, so does the essay in the *Yearbook* show that church discipline, "the rebuke," finds room in the context of the national church.

What Billing feared most of all was *codification* of church discipline.[36] When he deals with personal, human relations, he can always keep gift and demand, grace and judgment, mercy and righteousness together. We have pointed out many examples of this.[37] The commandment emerges naturally out of the unconditional gift of forgiveness, and works, which affect the relationships between men, grow naturally out of faith. But in this type of organization, in "the codes," there is no place for severity. It was as if Billing had forgotten that the territorial parish, which in its purely external form should express grace, the forgiveness of sins, is in all details governed by *codification.* Worship life in the parish church is indeed regulated by external statutes. Close by the parish church lies the free church mission house, which regards Matthew 18:15–17 as a code for the church law. The unity of gift and demand is lost in the types of organization. The gift is encapsulated in the codes of the parish church as decreed by the royal crown, and the demand is encapsulated in the codes of the free church approved by its members.

When this split of the ancient Christian unity took place, there was *one* code completely absent: the code permitting free and unconditional withdrawal, which was brought into being by the law granting religious freedom. Today we have this entirely new ordinance. Einar Billing was one of the most ardent advocates of such a law, although he did not live to see it enacted. Since this law of religious freedom has come, there is no reason why gift and demand should be divided between two different types of organization. The demand is becoming incorporated into the national church, and the gift appears more and more prominently in free church forms of activity.[38] It is not our purpose here to describe these changes that have taken place in Sweden since Billing's time. I have dealt with these matters in a couple of smaller pamphlets.[39]

### 3. A Comparison with Later Continental Theology

In his relationship with foreign countries, Billing was as one-sided as the majority of his countrymen. About the turn of the century the orientation was toward Germany, and as a young man Billing attended some German universities. Later in life he was invited there as guest lecturer, and he was also given honorary degrees from Greifswald, in 1917, and Marburg, in 1921.

The international theological development after 1945 surprisingly enough resulted in making theologians from Switzerland and Germany, especially older German theologians, the dominant leaders in practically all branches of modern theological scholarship. This is true even for England and the United States, even for Rome and Eastern Christianity. At the end of World War II no one could have reasonably expected such a development. This renaissance has also benefited two of Billing's great teachers, Martin Kähler (1835–1912) and Wilhelm Herrmann (1846–1922), whose works are now being reprinted and analyzed by respectful doctoral candidates. Even this outward situation indicates that Billing's thought-world was typically *modern.* After an interval of rest, his thought has suddenly become fully relevant.

It is not difficult to find one principal reason for this "return." During this past interim systematic theology strangely neglected the results of critical biblical scholarship as of no significance for its work. If we were to name the most important theological event between the Reformation of the sixteenth century and the present, there would be no hesitation in picking the candidate for first honors. The emergence of the historical view of the Bible during the nineteenth century was the most important event during this long period of 450 years. The critical examination of the Bible, the incorporation of the biblical word into the general literature of the world, and the study of it according to ordinary historical methods created at the beginning an enormous sensation in the churches. Billing belonged to this chaotic period, and "the great earthquake" of his youth was caused by his study of Wellhausen's *Prolegomena.*[40] But during the period we have called "the interim" there existed a strangely ambiguous attitude toward the historical view of the Bible. Almost everyone accepted it, but very few took it seriously. The churches consolidated themselves around certain centers: Lutheranism, Thomism, the *via media* of Anglicanism, and several others. In these attempts at consolidation the churches used the Bible as if historical biblical criticism did not exist. When the old theological warriors, those who were marked by scars of biblical criticism, and who all their lives took it seriously, now return during the 1960's, it is an indication that the interim period is at an end. As far as the churches are concerned, Vatican II may indeed mark the final breakthrough of "biblical criticism."

But Billing's works have not been translated into either German or English, and he has had no influence on continental theology. The parts of his works which have been translated are mere trifles; for example, *Our Calling (Vår kallelse),* forty-four pages; his guest lecture of 1927 at Königsberg, published in *Auslandsstudien* (1928), thirty-four pages; and, perhaps most important, an article in German on Herrmann's "Ethics," fifty-seven pages in *Zeitschrift für Theologie und Kirche* (1903).[41] Furthermore, most of these brief writings are difficult to understand for anyone who is unacquainted with Billing's larger works in Swedish. Since his work, from a methodological point of view, has not been continued nor even respected in the Swedish theology which followed him, Billing appears as a stranger in his encounter with modern continental theology. Later Swedish theological works have been translated into both German and English, sometimes quite undeservedly. It is difficult, therefore, to introduce Billing to a non-Swedish audience. Furthermore, he departed quite radically from his German teachers. To some extent, both Kähler and Herrmann reappear in Bultmann. But Billing is much more difficult to fit into the stalls that continental European theology has now constructed.

That which for Billing was vital we find today divided up into widely different tendencies in continental theology. This observation is at once obvious. Many different things, all vital, have become standards for the gathering of experts into different continental schools. Aspects and fragments have been identified with the whole, and have been set over against other fragments, which likewise have been identified with the whole in other contexts.

If we begin with Bultmann and demythologizing, Billing's similarity to Bultmann appears completely self-evident. In both we find a concentration on the New Testament kerygma as the central theme of the Bible, the kerygma concentrated in death and resurrection, the total concentration of Christ's work in soteriology, the interpretation of eschatology as a present reality, etc. But there are also other elements in Billing's special type of demythologizing which are completely incompatible with Bultmann's position. The prime examples are Jesus' messianic self-consciousness (essential, if his bestowal of the forgiveness of sins is to be historically comprehensible) and the Old Testament and the exodus as the essential pattern ("in the forgiveness of sins we live through our exodus from Egypt"). When we read these theses in Billing, we seem to be radically separated from Bultmann's program.[42] It seems sometimes that one is studying Gerhard von Rad instead, or some of the young German systematic theologians who have been influenced by his Old Testament exegesis— for example, Jürgen Moltmann, or Wolfhart Pannenberg. It could also be a rabbinically oriented exegesis of the New Testament, written by some modern German specialist on Jewish sources—such a one as is seldom mentioned in the footnotes of the Bultmann school. But in Billing all of these aspects are one.

If, again with the New Testament as the point of orientation, we turn our attention in the other direction, not back to the old Israel and its history, but forward to the Christian church and its worship, we can observe a number of parallels between Einar Billing and Oscar Cullmann. The geometrical pattern itself is the same for both. There is first a contracting perspective in the old covenant, then just one individual, Jesus, who vicariously takes upon himself the whole mission of Israel and carries it to his death on the cross. Then finally comes the sudden *expansion* of the lines toward "all nations" in the world mission of the church. The source of Billing's conception of the national church actually lies in his exegetical interpretation of the significance of Christ's resurrection.

For Billing the contracting line in the Old Testament and in Judaism is naturally not a "Christ-line" as Cullmann understands it. Billing follows an ordinary Old Testament exegesis and avoids all christological terms. But since the deliverance from Egypt and the passage through the Red Sea contribute the recurrent point of orientation, conceived of as an act of *election* and *grace,* and since this grace means an election of *the people* and cannot be individualized, the perspective must by inner necessity become narrower. The other product of the deliverance out of Egypt and the wandering through the wilderness, *the law,* can be individualized. Fewer and fewer individuals could pass the scrutiny of the law, and a diminishing number of pious Jews sustained the covenant. But none of these lowly individuals could find the act of *grace,* the act of election, in his own individual history. Grace lay embedded in the history of the people, in the history of their *origin,* which became more and more distant.[43] That history of Israel which surrounded the individual contained no grace; it was "a dark water" (2 Esdras, The Apocalypse of Baruch).[44] Billing described all this in the manner of an Old Testament exegete, with no christological interpretation. But the *expansion* after the resurrection of Christ is the same as in Cullmann's works. Here the texts from Paul indeed speak of Christ. Since the terms which Billing used to interpret the New Testament message were terms occurring in the *exodus,* the significance of Billing's interpretation becomes clear. What was intended in the election of *Israel* as a benefit for the whole world has now become realized in the act of Christ's resurrection and his encounter with individual after individual among all the nations of the world. Here only does the individual receive that "exodus from Egypt" which he could not find under the tyranny of the law in the history of Judaism. These are obvious similarities to Cullmann's well-known pattern. (In addition there are parallels in the interpretation of baptism, which I bypass here).

The similarity lies in the pattern, in the contraction and the expansion, and also in the conception of vicariousness which both Billing and Cullmann develop fully. On other points the differences are significant. If hypothetically we were to strike out Billing's concept of "the individual," it would not be possible within Billing's pattern to explain how the contraction and the expansion proceed. That the demand of the law became individualized but grace did *not* is the salient point which explains the process of contraction, or the Old Testament development. That the grace of election became individualized when Jesus gave forgiveness of sins to the individual, and that the same forgiveness in a similar individualistic form is now given to individuals among "all nations" through the already operating world mission—this is Billing's salient point in regard to the expansion, or the New Testament development. Billing described both of these developments by using normal exegetical and critical methods. The one is a completely "unpneumatic" Old Testament exegesis, the other is a rather ordinary New Testament exegesis.[45] But what happens to the *individual* is the fundamental question, the determinative element in the pattern. And this question is not at all typical for Cullmann. He can describe the time line as a Christ-line without this reference to the individual. He does not have such a specific form of anthropology in his hermeneutical apparatus.

Here we are back to our starting point: Billing's similarity to Bultmann. We are back, but only to discover new and surprising features in Billing's theology which make it difficult to place him within the present continental situation. Bultmann's anthropology is the anthropology of one certain philosopher, in a specific book published in 1927. Einar Billing, who was eighteen years older than Martin Heidegger, had already developed his fundamental point of view when *Sein und Zeit* appeared. He could not possibly have been influenced by a work issued at that late date. But, just like Herrmann and Kähler, who were strongly influenced by nineteenth century German philosophy, he could have found among his contemporaries a philosophical apparatus if he had sought for it, and he could have built up an anthropology with its help. Since the individual plays this dominant role as hermeneutical principle in the interpretation of scripture, he ought to have "a need for philosophy" somewhere in the system. Billing was competent in this area, as his chapter on Greek philosophy in his *The Ethical Thoughts (De etiska tankarna)* clearly shows, not to mention his other contributions to the history of philosophy.[46] But in the center of his biblical theology there is not a trace of it. Here Einar Billing reminds us most vividly of Karl Barth. Like him he is driven by a strong theological purism and manifests an *indifference* to "points of contact" that seems rather strange.

But neither does the comparison with Barth lead anywhere. It is true in a sense that Billing operated with the order, "gospel and law." The election comes first, then the commandment. First the deliverance from Egypt, then the Decalogue. But the word which in the resurrection of Christ goes out into the world and establishes the national churches is conceived of exclusively as "the forgiveness of sins." One almost has to be a specialist on Judaism, it would seem, in order to understand how the divinity of Christ expresses itself in the word of forgiveness more clearly than in anything else. Billing's description of Jesus' historical situation is so filled with local Jewish color, and the atmosphere of conflict between Jesus and the Pharisees is so specialized, that one would need a little extra anthropology to make this strictly localized word into a gospel, "a good news," to *all* nations. Here Billing presupposed that every man in every culture stands under *the law*, but he was satisfied to assume silently this dominion of the law. He never systematically developed the connection between creation and law. Even though he made the presupposition silently, the difference between Barth and him appears just as definite. We cannot place Billing in the Barthian fold, either.

If through the forgiveness of sins Jesus gave the individual Israelite the same "exodus" as the people received through the deliverance out of Egypt, then, in the first place, the presupposition is that the tyranny of the law in the conscience is the individual's "house of bondage." If in the preaching of the gospel Jesus now goes "from nation to nation" in order to

142                                   *An Exodus Theology*

deal with new individuals as he did in Galilee, then, in the second place, it is presupposed that Judaism's "house of bondage," guilt, is the torment of every man.[47] Without these two presuppositions the whole frame of Billing's structure crumbles. But, we repeat, this is presupposed, not explicitly stated. Billing must have known guilt as something self-evident, just as for the physician sickness lies embedded permanently in existence. The physician may search for remedies, medicine, therapy, and means of care. But in "points of contact" he is not at all interested. He would not even deign to answer if a person should remark to him: "You seem to presuppose without question that sickness exists."

NOTES TO CHAPTER VI

1. All three of these articles, together with previous writings (from 1911 to 1926) have now been published in the second edition of *Den svenska folkkyrkan* (Stockholm, 1963), pp. 65–186.

2. See the letter from K. B. Westman (1908) in Olle Nystedt, *Från Studentkorståget till Sigtunastiftelsen,* (Stockholm, 1936), pp. 97 f. Cf. Gerda Billing, *Den oförglömliga prästgården* (Stockholm, 1950), pp. 96, 159, *et passim*.

3. It is significant that Olle Nystedt dedicated his 1936 work on the young church movement to the following three men: J. A. Eklund, Einar Billing, and Manfred Björkquist. The first two were then still serving as bishops. Björkquist was Bishop of Stockholm from 1942 to 1954, Olle Nystedt being then dean of the Stockholm cathedral and *Pastor Primarius*.

4. Cf. Nystedt, *op. cit.,* p. 33.

5. Note the frequently quoted passage in *Den Svenska folkkyrkan,* p. 142 (Lecture at the Pastoral Conference of 1937). It is well known that Billing approved of democratic order in the Church without regarding this as decisive for its character as a national church. Rather, he regarded the geographical nature of the territorial parish as fundamental because this form expressed the activity of the gospel as directed toward *all* men. (*Den svenska folkkyrkan,* pp. 50–56, 133–42).

6. This appears especially in the unpublished part of the work. See Gösta Wrede, *Kyrkosynen i Einar Billings teologi* (Stockholm, 1966), pp. 60–63.

7. *Den svenska folkkyrkan,* pp. 68–74, 83 f.

8. *Ibid.,* pp. 114 f.; cf. pp. 123 f.

9. *Ibid.*, p. 127 (italics mine). See also Einar Billing, *Guds närhet* (2nd ed.; Stockholm, 1949), pp. 35 f.

10. Cf. *Den svenska folkkyrkan*, pp. 152–86. In regard to Billing's attitude toward the problem of the pastor's duty to officiate at the wedding ceremony see also Olof Sundby, *Luthersk äktenskapsuppfattning* (Stockholm, 1959), pp. 222–27, 300 f.

11. It is significant that Nygren wrote his doctoral thesis in the area of philosophy of religion (*Religiöst apriori* [Lund, 1921]), and thus even in his initial research took up a problem which Billing during his whole life left untouched, i.e., the relationship between theology and philosophy.

12. Cf. Gustaf Aulén, *Den kristna gudsbilden* (Stockholm, 1927), pp. 360 f.; also *Hundra års svensk kyrkodebatt* (Stockholm, 1953), pp. 79–115; and "Nathan Söderblom och Einar Billing—kontraster i samverkan," *Svensk teologisk kvartalskrift* (1962), pp. 205–23.

13. Later, however, during his years as bishop, Runestam became a warm supporter of Billing's conception of the national church.

14. When Aulén describes the situation in Uppsala at the turn of the century, he is anxious to keep these two, Söderblom and Billing, together. We note this as early as *Den kristna gudsbilden* (Stockholm, 1927), pp. 358–61, 379 n. 1. This point recurs frequently in Aulén's later works. It is also important to note that Lundensian theology also extended participation in ecumenical work.

15. The collection of essays issued in 1942 under the title *En bok om kyrkan* reflects this trend. (Anders Nygren [ed.], *This Is the Church*, trans. Carl C. Rasmussen [Philadelphia: Fortress Press, 1952].) Hjalmar Lindroth, who had been greatly influenced by Aulén, followed the trend and edited another collection of essays, *En bok om kyrkans ämbete* (Stockholm, 1951), but without any Lundensian contributions.

16. Cf. the criticism of Billing by Ragnar Bring, *Till frågan om den systematiska teologiens uppgift* I (Lund, 1933), pp. 130–58.

17. Billing defined his opposition to the later Lundensian theology in his lecture, "Idealism and Christianity," at Sigtuna in 1934. The manuscript (51 typewritten pages) is now in the University Library in Lund.

18. See G. Törnvall, *Andligt och världsligt regemente* (Stockholm, 1940), pp. ix, 1–4. The author refers constantly to Billing. See also Gustaf Wingren, *Luther on Vocation*, trans. Carl C. Rasmussen (Philadelphia: Fortress Press, 1957), pp. 74 f.

19. See the previous section, IV:1, "The Doctrine of the Two Realms."

20. Cf. Einar Billing, "Från biskop Gottfrid Billings Västeråstid," *Julbok för Västerås stift* (1925), p. 33. Billing himself used the term "high church" with regard to the neo-Lutheranism in the state church of the nineteenth century, a usage which is not relevant today.

21. E.g., George S. Hendry, *The Holy Spirit in Christian Theology* (Philadelphia: Westminister Press, 1956), p. 74.

22. It would be well to reread *Den svenska folkkyrkan,* pp. 101–64, from this point of view, especially the two first fundamental articles from 1911 and 1926.

23. Cf. the Emmaus sermon in *Guds närhet,* pp. 74–76; also Billing's reflections on confirmation and the eucharist in *Den svenska folkkyrkan,* pp. 176–80 (Lecture at the 1937 Pastoral Conference).

24. Yngve Brilioth, *Eucharistic Faith and Practice,* trans. A. G. Hebert (New York: Macmillan Co., 1931).

25. For the following discussion see Billing's exegesis of "the church discipline passage" (Matt. 18:15–17) in *Guds närhet,* pp. 98–105, a passage to which we shall return later. (Originally this was an article from 1922.)

26. Einar Billing, *De etiska tankarna i urkristendomen* (2nd ed. enlarged; Stockholm, 1936), pp. 389 f. (most italics mine). Cf. *Guds närhet,* pp. 101–3.

27. See C. H. Lyttkens and V. Vajta (eds.), *Church in Fellowship* (Minneapolis: Augsburg Publishing Concern, 1965), pp. 181–88.

28. "Grundtvigs og Einar Billings syn på folkekirken," *Viborgs stifts årbog* (1949), pp. 128–44. Grundtvig differs from Billing at two points. Grundtvig has a *theological* theory of what it means to be a human being, and he regards the Danish national church simply as "a civil institution," which as such is "expedient." The difference between these two has influenced the history of the church in Denmark and Sweden.

29. Gerda Billing, *op. cit.,* pp. 35–42, 50, 83–87, 94–97, 127.

30. *Ibid.,* pp. 41 f., passages from a letter from Einar Billing to his home in Lund, Aug. 1, 1910. (Italics mine.)

31. Billing served as chief pastor in Hagby and Ramsta from 1908 to 1918, which was precisely the time when he developed his conception of the church.

32. See Bengt Hallgren, *Kyrkotuktsfrågan* (Lund, 1963), pp. 231–40.

33. See *Guds närhet,* pp. 99–103.

34. *Ibid.,* pp. 103 f. Cf. *De etiska tankarna,* p. 390.

35. *Guds närhet,* pp. 104 f. (italics mine); cf. pp. 99 f.

36. *Ibid.,* p. 105; also 100, 103.

37. Several examples are given in sections above, most clearly in these: III.4, "Death and Resurrection"; IV.1, "The Doctrine of the Two Realms"; IV.2, "The Forgiveness of Sins"; and V, "Unresolved Tensions."

38. What Billing, in his last lecture at the 1937 Pastoral Conference, called his "will and testament' was a *warning* to the national church. It is well to remember this. The great danger was that the church would lose its *message* and begin to think of itself as "subject" (*Den svenska folkkyrkan,* pp. 185 f.). But the demand lies always embedded in the message.

39. Gustaf Wingren, *Demokrati i folkkyrkan* (Lund, 1963), *Folk-kyrkotanken* ([Stockholm, 1964], see pp. 33–39), and also, e.g., such articles as "Fram mot en enad kyrka" (*Tro och liv* [1967]), pp. 3–10.

40. See again Einar Billing, *Herdabrev till prästerskapet i Västerås stift* (2nd ed.; Stockholm, 1962), pp. 46–48.

41. Einar Billing, "Etische Grundfragen des evangelisches Christentums," *Zeitschr. f. Theol. u. Kirche* (1903), pp. 267–323. This was originally written in German.

42. This becomes clear when one analyzes section III.4 above, "Death and Resurrection."

43. Cf. *De etiska tankarna,* pp. 154, 197–99, 219, 264.

44. *Ibid.,* pp. 194 f., 197, 221.

45. See above, III.2–4, where his fundamental biblical theology has been described in detail. Each one of these sections describes the several parts of the process. The narrowing line is described in "The People (Grace) and the Individual (Law)," the turning point comes in "Jesus and the Individual," the expansion follows in "Death and Resurrection." This outline provides the basis for the next section, III.5, "The Nature of the National Church." This last, too, is placed in the context of biblical theology, and it precedes the discussion of Billing's works on Luther. Such a presentation of Billing's biblical theology shows clearly the similarities between Cullmann and him, but also the differences.

46. See *De etiska tankarna,* pp. 19–76, and in addition, e.g., his extensive discussion of the Aristotelianism of Rudbeckius (1923).

47. Cf. Einar Billing, *I katekesundervisningens tjänst* (2nd ed.; Stockholm, 1943), pp. 132–58, and also the whole conception of the forgiveness of sins as a gift from the church to the people, as Billing developed it, especially in the two first chapters of *Den svenska folkkyrkan.*

# CHAPTER VII

# A NEGLECTED PROBLEM:
## THE RELATIONSHIP BETWEEN THEOLOGY AND PHILOSOPHY

### 1. The Actual Lacuna

Billing introduced his theme in *The Ethical Thoughts (De etiska tankarna)* with the following words:

> In almost every moral judgment we "moderns" make, in nearly every ethical concept we use, in practically every ideal we set up to strive for, we will discover on closer analysis *two* fundamental and dominant elements, although there may also be several others from other sources. These two main elements point back, each to its own great line of development in the cultural history of humanity. One has its roots in Hellenistic culture, in Greek philosophy, in the intellectual work of Socrates, Plato, and the Stoics. The other element brings us back through the history of the Christian church to that history to which the Old and the New Testaments bear witness. . . . It is marvelous to contemplate how these two lines of development ran parallel through the centuries without knowledge or consciousness of one another, and how they have since begun to meet more and more frequently, first at the beginning of Christianity and then throughout the history of the church. And finally they have coalesced so completely that even with the help of a sharp analysis it is difficult to determine what originally belonged to the one or to the other.[1]

These statements imply that the biblical word and classical Greek philosophy constitute components in almost every ethical affirmation a modern European makes. But Billing never attempted to substantiate these propositions in any way. These statements are found on the first page of Billing's principal work, which covers 440 pages, but not once in this

146

whole presentation does he consider one typically modern ethical affirmation to prove his thesis. In spite of the fact that his subsequent literary activity extended from the publication of *The Ethical Thoughts* in 1907 to his death in 1939, he never returned in any other writing to an analysis that would have supported his contention.

The relationship between theology and philosophy belongs among the subjects which Billing never discussed. In his work of 1907 there is, as we have noted earlier, a chapter on ethical thought in Greek philosophy from the Sophists to Socrates, Plato, Aristotle, the Epicureans, the Stoics, and finally Neoplatonism. In this chapter Billing had occasion to consider several works of prominent contemporary philosophers, especially Germans. It was then more common than now that a philosopher wrote studies in the history of philosophy. These were generally devoted to a study of the old Greeks, and were sometimes heavily colored by the brand of philosophy the nineteenth century author himself represented. Rudolph Eucken appears several times (for example, pp. 30, 49, and 75), as does Axel Hägerström (pp. 42, 46). Wilhelm Windelband is mentioned and quoted throughout, and a specialist like Eduard Zeller is quite significant (pp. 39, 68–70).[2] But as far as direct references and discussions are concerned, the part these philosophers played ended when Billing finished the chapter on Greek philosophy. When he took up the Old Testament, the references, both in footnotes and in the text, were to exegetes and historians of religion. Billing's only purpose was to compare two phenomena from the past: the philosophers of Greece and the prophets in Israel. The purpose of such a descriptive comparison was indeed to perform a task relevant to the present, namely, the interpretation of the biblical word for men today. But in this interpretation, in which he made use of such present-day institutions as the parish church, the territorial parish, etc., Billing presented no confrontation between the gospel and philosophy. He referred in his discussion to natural science, more frequently to the labor movement, and most often to the free churches—but not to philosophy.[3]

As Billing strove to perform the actual task which he had assumed, the interpretation of the biblical word for the present time, he also pursued an apologetic line of thought. Here he affirmed that the prophetic unity of righteousness and mercy can be shown to be superior to those types of ethos that were developed by the Greek philosophers. But even here he merely defined the task in *The Ethical Thoughts*; within this work itself we look mostly in vain for any presentation of proofs of this superiority.[4] What Billing in his historical analysis actually said about this subject was essentially that the biblical type of ethos is more vigorous, more adaptable to changing situations, etc. But in his attempt to interpret the biblical material in this close connection with life he could certainly have been influenced by some current philosophy of life. Ragnar Bring, who in his critical study of Billing sought to establish a tendency toward "a metaphysic of the will," and who pointed out parallels especially with Kant and Herrmann, insisted that such an influence could readily be detected.[5]

The influence of contemporary philosophy on the interpretation of the Bible has operated throughout the whole history of Christian ideology, very likely without exception as far as significant theologians are concerned. It would be surprising if Billing should have been an exception to this general rule. But it is much more interesting to observe the opposite phenomenon in Billing's case. He refused to deal with the relationship between philosophy and theology, and constantly avoided this task. In this respect he has few equals, among whom is Barth. Naturally, this does not mean that Billing and Barth have not been influenced by philosophy. But neither one of them presents first an interpretation of "human existence" (Bultmann), or of "the human mind" (Nygren), in order afterwards to incorporate *into it* the result of their biblical interpretation derived from their exegetical work. Barth has again and again given reasons for avoiding this method. Billing simply left the problem alone, silently and passively.

But in some respects he spoke out clearly and intentionally, as, for instance, in expressing his disapproval of Hägerström and Nygren. The latter had early declared his agreement with Hägerström in print, especially on the very vital point regarding the function of ethics.[6] In the unpublished lecture of 1934, on idealism and Christianity, in which Billing appraised Lundensian theology, he particularly questioned this attachment to Hägerström's philosophy.[7] It is possible that the cause of Billing's negative attitude was, to some extent, Hägerström's meddling with theological affairs at Uppsala, especially in connection with doctoral disputations and the appointment of professors. In at least three of his letters to Lund in the year 1918 Billing reported on Hägerström.[8] But his aversion to the easy acceptance of a rather questionable philosophical program by the theologians at Lund had deeper roots in his own theological *principles*. He was afraid that some essential theological values would be lost because of this contact.

## 2. The Unexpressed Presuppositions

The theologically relevant points in Billing's unpublished lecture, "Idealism and Christianity" ("Idealism och kristendom"), serve to explain his passive and hesitant attitude toward contemporary philosophy. The most important element threatened by the connection with Hägerström was, according to Billing, the conception of *conscience*. Here he quoted directly Romans 2:14 f., and mentioned in the same context both Kant and Herrmann with critical approval.[9] What Billing feared most of all was the conception that systems of value are to be regarded positivistically as actual historical entities connected with certain groups of like-minded people, and that these systems have thus been developed in different cultural situations. Christianity can then be regarded as *one* of these systems, characterized by agape and comparable to other systems of value which have a different orientation. In this context essential elements of *the Christian faith* itself become lost, strangely enough in the very description of "what is specifically Christian." The universal elements are lost: God's work with the whole creation and his work with every man, whether he is a Christian or not. Conscience stands guard in order to preserve the universal aspect. Billing charged that Lundensian theology was apathetic toward the interpretation of "conscience" and that this apathy had its roots in the acceptance of a contemporary Swedish philosophy (from Uppsala). Billing regarded this situation with "consternation."[10]

The other point in Billing's criticism is rather surprising, since it involved a certain self-correction. He picked for discussion Romans 8:18–39, on "the groaning of creation," which he regarded as a fundamentally important biblical text. It was primarily Nygren's description of "eros" which caused him to focus on this human activity *"from below."* The Bible assumes that man moves upward toward God. "The inmost element in creation is prayer," and creation groans in its bondage. Billing often dealt with prayer, and he developed almost the whole subject in his *Pastoral Letter (Herdabrev)*. But there was a new, somewhat self-critical accent in "Idealism and Christianity," an emphasis on *creation*.[11] It is therefore characteristic that he considered, albeit in passing, "the image of God" according to the New Testament, a theme which otherwise played a very minor role in his published works.[12] The terms "image" and "likeness," taken from the narrative of creation in Genesis, were used by both the church fathers and Luther in associating anthropology and Christology, creation and redemption. This usage is absent in Nygren's works, and notably absent even in his description of concrete, historical sources (for example, Irenaeus).[13] When Billing in this 1934 manuscript discussed "the image of God" together with "the groaning of creation" and "the conscience" of the Gentiles (Rom. 2:14 f.), these features all point in the same direction.

But in what direction? We have already suggested that Billing's thought-structure was open in one direction in which he himself refused to advance. This is really paradoxical, because such an advance would have involved a further development of some of his most beloved ideas. That "image" and "likeness" occupied such a modest place in Billing's published works was due to the fact that baptism as a union with Christ in death and resurrection was such a peripheral point in his teaching. We have to go to Paul in order to find the relevant New Testament texts on "image" and "likeness," and we have to find them in Paul's *teaching about baptism.* These New Testament passages are pregnant with an ordinary, everyday ethos. Paul's whole ethical teaching rests on "the following" of Christ in death and resurrection. On the basis of such passages Billing could have developed his whole original unity of righteousness and mercy in an *ethical* context, which he had done earlier very skillfully in respect to both Israel's prophetism and the Synoptic Gospels. But he never dealt in depth with these Pauline passages, due partly to the selection of subject in *The Atonement (Försoningen),* published in 1908, and partly to his unique construction of the conception of the national church in the years immediately following.[14] In the pattern of the national church the crucial point was *infant* baptism, the sign of prevenient grace. But Billing's structure was *open* in other directions, as we can see in his diligent work on the unity of righteousness and mercy, gift and demand, etc. But after his definitive development of a structure for his conception of the national church he found an expression for this unity only in meditative and homiletical addresses to the individual. In the pattern of organization the unity of gift and demand fell apart. In its "codes" the territorial congregation can articulate the gift, but not the demand.[15]

*This* lacuna in the center of Billing's theology is connected with a more special lacuna to which we have just referred: the absence of any independent discussion of "creation and law." In "Idealism and Christianity" (1934) he opened all avenues in that direction by mentioning the image of God, the universal law among all nations, and the groaning of creation, but he took no steps in that direction. He remained in his purely "ecclesiastical" structure. His affinity with the later high church movement lies perhaps in this confinement within the walls of the temple. (The principal section of the lecture of 1934 consisted of quotations from J. O. Wallin's *Psalmbok* of 1819, very sympathetically analyzed.)[16] But an excursus into the subject of creation and law would have caused a number of modifications in Billing's system. It would have provided a new conception of baptism (death and resurrection, not exclusively prevenient grace), a different view of work in the calling (the world and the law, not forgiveness of sins), and especially an entirely new emphasis in *the conception of the church*.[17] The relation of the church to creation, the church as "restoration," the recapitulation of *the human,* would then have received a much greater emphasis than it actually did in his work.[18]

From the point of view of biblical theology, all these "lacunae" stem from his starting point in Exodus and his almost total neglect of Genesis. Israel appears to be elected out of a vacuum, "the nations," and the church seems to lie in a theological vacuum, "the people." But the word of forgiveness goes out *to* all humanity, the first word that transcends Israel and addresses itself to all. The Swedish national church brings forgiveness of sins to the Swedish people.[19] In this context Billing's obvious presuppositions are (1) humanity as a creation and (2) a conscience weighed down by guilt. These obvious presuppositions in Billing's theology would very likely have been more clearly articulated in his work as a whole, as Gösta Wrede has suggested, if the second part of his doctoral dissertation, *Luther's Teaching Concerning the State (Luthers lära om staten)*, had been published.[20] It is available now only in a beautifully typed manuscript. With its starting point in Luther's conception of the law, this manuscript points in the same direction as the unpublished lecture of 1934, "Idealism and Christianity."

Billing's situation in regard to the problem he left out of the discussion, the relationship between philosophy and theology, is therefore perfectly clear. The presuppositions of all his work involved an anthropology in which the concepts of creation and guilt were fundamental. If he had at all entered the area between philosophy and theology, these *universal* elements would have furnished the main problems for his analytical work: conscience, the law as dominant over all men, etc. Billing stood in a general cultural situation in which the old idealistic philosophy of German vintage had begun to disappear and a modern analytical philosophy was appearing. One of the pioneers of this new thought was Axel Hägerström, who was connected with Billing's university, Uppsala. Billing was sufficiently familiar with this newer philosophy to know that the *universal* elements, the elements concerned with creation and law in the biblical texts, would become lost in an eventual cooperation with a philosophy structured according to this pattern. He found proof of this danger in the obvious situation at Lund, where, with Anders Nygren as the leader, theology had even in the 1920's accepted certain of Hägerström's theses, and as a result had lost all possibilities of describing even historically these *universal* elements. The Lundensian motif research presented instead a description of specific Christian elements: agape, Christology, justification, etc. Billing had no interest in this narrow concentration. He regarded it as dangerous. He had never encountered any philosophy other than idealism and the philosophy of Hägerström. His only escape was to leave the whole problem of philosophy and theology outside the discussion.[21] The real lacunae in his work at this central point are thereby explained.

But an additional explanation can be found in certain internal factors in Billing's *theology,* in the spontaneous choice he made in his study of both the biblical material and the sixteenth century sources. The concept of creation had a relatively insignificant role. It was, to be sure, present everywhere, but characteristically enough it was *presupposed.* When he sometimes presented it, it was done in passing, while the main theme was always the *exodus.* That the Bible begins with Genesis was for Billing a rather insignificant fact. The same attitude prevailed in his treatment of Luther. The worldly kingdom was of little importance, but Billing's rhetoric began to sparkle when he spoke of the *church.*[22]

### 3. The Neglect of the Doctrine of Creation

The wounds which a man receives in his youth never completely disappear. The scars left by Billing's encounter with Wellhausen can be seen in his whole literary production, from beginning to end. Wellhausen's criticism of the church's traditional view of the Pentateuch had been directed largely against the conception of a verbally inspired literary production by an author, Moses, who stood "apart from history." What Wellhausen demolished was the dream of five holy books whose origin was fundamentally different from anything within a normal historical process. What he constructed instead was a sketch of a very common literary process of writing. First a number of unexpected events took place (deliverance, exodus, the wandering in the wilderness). Men began to ponder the significance of these events, and human authors recorded these thoughts and the events in their books. Billing's great achievement was that he accepted Wellhausen's total reconstruction (which, on the particular point we are dealing with here, has not become antiquated by later research). It is, said Billing, an advantage for the church and present-day preaching that the doctrine of verbal inspiration has disappeared. Now finally the important role of the events can become clear. Billing understood Golgotha and the empty tomb as an extension of the Pentateuch, as a new development of the same biblical paradigm: first, something which no one expected happened; then, "the word" emerged from the event. This was the word of the gospel that went out from Jerusalem and established the church in nation after nation.[23]

But if this is the pattern, then the narrative of creation becomes a somewhat disturbing text, even from a purely literary point of view. Whatever "creation" may be, it can under no possible circumstances be an historical event on a par with the exodus out of Egypt and the crucifixion on Golgotha. Here we face another blunder caused by the doctrine of inspiration. It assumed that the narrative of creation described an historical sequence. Really the opposite is true. When a people in history have experienced a deliverance like the redemption out of Egypt, that people will project their experience on nature, the starry heavens, and the course of the world. In this secondary sense "a story of creation" originated. In making that projection, this people did not really add anything to their primary experience of exodus. They simply thought through what the exodus out of Egypt and the passage through the Red Sea really meant. Of course Yahweh could not have brought this little elected people out of powerful Egypt unless he governed *everything*—wind and wave, light and darkness, sickness and health, life and death. Thus the narrative of creation proclaims God's dominion over *everything.* The purpose of this text is to bring the course of the whole world and the life and death of all creatures into a relationship with God the Creator. But if we understand the literary origin of the story of creation in this way (and that is what Billing did), the idea of creation plays a relatively minor role.[24] It is there, but it has no independent claim. It is a by-product of "the exodus," and it has to rest on historical events if it is to stay alive. Exodus can stand on its own right, but Genesis cannot.

This conception remained Billing's fundamental point of view. As a result "the universal elements" (conscience, the image of God, the universal law among the Gentiles), which we discussed in the previous section, remained as "assumed presuppositions." Only when these universal elements were *threatened* did Billing try to articulate these presuppositions, which up to that time he had assumed as self-evident. He held that they were threatened by the junction of Hägerström and Nygren during the 1920's and 1930's, and his lecture, "Idealism and Christianity," was an answer to this threat.[25] But by that time Billing's literary production was practically completed. In his large original writings from 1900 to 1920 these universal elements occupied a less prominent position. The exodus and the church had the primary place, not creation and human life as such.

If we turn to Billing's treatment of Luther, we encounter at once a similar situation. Aside from the rather few passages in the New Testament which speak of "emperor," "government," "soldiers," etc., the biblical texts which were relevant for Luther were from the Old Testament. In fact, the foundation of his teaching about the state is Genesis, and especially the first chapters of this book, the so-called prehistorical section. Billing, who wrote *Luther's Teaching Concerning the State* and consequently was an expert on this subject, recorded faithfully, as an expert would do, everything that was typical in Luther's teaching. He said that the first pages of Genesis were the starting point, that the civil and ceremonial regulations in the Mosaic law applied to the Jews and not to any other people, and that the Decalogue applies to all of us since it is an expression of "natural law." Everything that needed to be said about the universality of the law according to Luther was recorded clearly and succinctly in Billing's doctoral thesis of 1900.[26] But *nothing* of this which he had seen and very clearly stated played any significant role in what he later wrote about Luther's positive significance as an interpreter of the Bible *for men of today*. What Billing said in *Our Calling (Vår kallelse)* with regard specifically to Luther's doctrine of the call applies here in general: "Of course, it is not merely a return to Luther, it cannot and may not be this."[27] We in the present are "expressing what Luther left implied in his doctrine of the call."[28] As we have noted earlier (in IV.1 above, "The Doctrine of the Two Realms") this correction meant that Luther's two realms, earth and heaven, tended to become *one,* with the forgiveness of sins as the principle governing the whole. This was a new victory of Exodus over Genesis even in the interpretation of Luther.[29]

One of the delightful facts about great theologians is that they never make a mistake. They never do anything without knowing what they are doing. Some have thought that Billing's book, *In the Service of Catechetical Instruction (I katekesundervisningens tjänst),* represented a departure and an accommodation to the traditional pattern (creation and law before exodus and redemption). This is, however, not the case. This catechetical work was primarily an examination of previous textbooks for confirmation instruction. It was necessary, therefore, for Billing to conform to the order of the five parts in Luther's Catechisms (the Decalogue before the Creed, the first article before the second, etc.). The books which Billing examined naturally followed this order. But as soon as a mod-

ern author of textbooks began to attribute a fundamental
significance to this order, Billing at once raised objections
against such an argument. He rejected it decisively, even
though his opponent was to some extent closer to Luther. (In
the *Large Catechism* Luther presented certain arguments in
favor of the traditional order which he had followed).[30] It is
indeed quite clear that the particular Swedish textbook which
Billing examined (by J. Johansson) was not able to express
what Luther intended. Billing's criticism was therefore justi-
fied.[31] But it is also clear that Billing's thought differed from
Luther, and that he went his own way on the basis of his
start in biblical theology with exodus and forgiveness of sins.
In his catechetical work (first published in 1913), that starting
point drove him to rather critical views of the traditional
conception of conscience, while in contrast he seems to have
accepted that view in his unpublished lecture of 1934, "Idealism and Christianity."[32]

But when Billing was not compelled to *choose* between
Exodus and Genesis, and when he could operate in the *neutral*
area of biblical theology and ecclesiology, he could allow the
thought of creation a separate and independent existence. It
was so at the beginning of his literary work, and it remained
so to the end.[33] A good example of this line of thought is
found in his article on the freedom of all scientific research
and on the conviction of faith that free science serves God's
purpose most adequately. In that context he could speak of
the doctrine of *creation* as "a bond" between all sciences, and
especially between theology and all the other disciplines.

> From this point of view the bond between it and the other sciences
> has not been relaxed but rather tied more securely. It cannot be
> stated more succinctly than it is in the motto of Uppsala Uni-
> versity: *gratiae veritas naturae. Faith in creation ties the bond
> together.* In this view theology must not only allow but demand
> that the investigation of all areas of reality shall proceed in free-
> dom from all laws except those imposed by reality itself. Along

this line lies the guarantee of an ultimate unity. Theology knows that conflicts . . . must inevitably arise, but on the basis of its certainty that the world is God's world it can regard them . . . only as anachronisms. And when the other sciences with almost anxious zeal defend their freedom, it recognizes in this concern an element of its own nature. Although this is seldom acknowledged, the Reformation with its insistence on personal faith has contributed more to this point of view than has the Renaissance.[34]

What modern secularizing theology, following Friedrich Gogarten's lead, has had to say about the roots of secularism in the Reformation and especially in its doctrine of creation contains nothing much that is new in comparison with these lines Billing wrote before World War I.[35] (Gogarten is, after all, more than anyone else the pioneer in this area.) But we must note that such statements stand relatively isolated in Billing's works. In general it was not the doctrine of creation and the common human experiences that occupied his theological thought.

There were two earlier attacks that tied him down to exodus and the conception of the church. These were, first, Wellhausen's criticism of the Pentateuch and, second, the free churches' criticism of the territorial congregation. In both cases Billing accepted the criticisms and did not dismiss them. He sought to find positive meaning in the Old Testament on the premise that the origin of these books was related to and dependent upon historical events, a premise which Wellhausen had somewhat triumphantly clarified. He sought, likewise, to find meaning in the territorial parishes on the premise that they must have these external, geographical boundaries about which Waldenström spoke so scornfully.[36] But a people's departure from a country on the map, Egypt, and a parish church with a definite area on the map are not entities which we in our cultural climate can connect with "philosophy." The relationship between theology and philosophy would have appeared quite different if Billing had analyzed his unexpressed presuppositions and, for example, had given a precise meaning to his own formulation, "the boundaries which life itself establishes."[37] The unexpressed thought implied in that statement is that human life itself (not only the life of Israel and the church) is *created* and has a certain inescapable *structure* that cannot be dislocated without destroying life. If there is such a structure, it can be observed quite independently of faith. If one takes the thought of creation seriously, one cannot in the long run avoid dealing with the relationship between philosophy and theology.

### NOTES TO CHAPTER VII

1. Einar Billing, *De etiska tankarna i urkristendomen* (2nd ed. enlarged; Stockholm, 1936), p. 9.

2. Billing makes no claim to originality in this chapter. See *ibid.*, p. 18 n. 1.

3. In regard to natural science, cf. *ibid.*, pp. 25–90. Even here Eucken plays a dominant role (pp. 253–60). This chapter, which deals with the historical background of the concept of "natural law," is now a part of the second edition of *De etiska tankarna*, but was originally published in a volume honoring Pehr Eklund (1911).

4. See, however, *De etiska tankarna*, pp. 74 f.

5. Ragnar Bring, *Till frågan om den systematiska teologiens uppgift* (Lund, 1933), pp. 133–36, and in several other places. Cf. Billing's brief book, *Den uppriktige och Gud*, (2nd ed.; Uppsala, 1917), pp. 16 f. (Bring follows mostly Adolph Phalén, a colleague of Hägerström in the philosophy department at Uppsala.)

6. See Anders Nygren, "Det etiska omdömets självständighet," *Svensk teol. kvartalskrift* (1925), p. 39. (In other contexts Nygren could also raise objections to Hägerström).

7. See "Idealism och kristendom" (unpublished; 1934), pp. 8–10. (The manuscript is in the University Library in Lund).

8. The letters in question are from May 24, Nov. 29 (discussion with Arthur Engberg), and Dec. 13 of 1918 (see Gerda Billing, *Fjärran Upsalaår* [Stockholm, 1955], pp. 25 f., 89 f., and 93). The debate in Uppsala during the night in November of 1918, with Engberg representing Hägerström's philosophy, evidently dealt with "the central question of the theory of knowledge" (*ibid.*, p. 89). But Einar Billing did not think it meaningful to discuss this question in a letter to his father, the Bishop of Lund, or to seek to explain the significance of the question: "It doesn't pay to pursue this matter" (*ibid.*, p. 89).

9. "Idealism och kristendom," pp. 36–39 (he quotes the biblical text, but the reference is not given). Bring's reference to Kant and Herrmann (*op. cit.*, pp. 133–58) points therefore in the right direction.

10. "Idealism och kristendom," p. 38. Cf. the reference to Hägerström's "tetanus germ," *ibid.*, p. 10.

11. *Ibid.*, pp. 46–51; cf. *Herdabrev*, pp. 131–36.

12. "Idealism och kristendom," p. 33.

13. Gen. 1:26. Cf. my article in *Svensk teol. kvartalskrift* (1940), p. 155; also p. 151. Nygren dealt with Irenaeus for the first time in 1936, although his analysis was based on the concept of agape, which he had developed as early as 1930. It is from this description that Billing argues.

14. See above, III.4, "Death and Resurrection," where the subject is fully developed.

15. Cf. above, IV.3, "The Territorial Parish and the Individual," and VI.2c, "Opposition to the Free Churches."

16. See above, VI.2b, "The High Church Tendency."

17. A detailed account of most of these points is found in IV.1 above, "The Doctrine of the Two Realms."

18. See the introductory section on biblical theology, III.1 above, "Greece and the Prophets." Billing shares the weakness of the free church, since the first article is relatively meaningless.

19. See above, III.5, "The Nature of the National Church," and especially VI.3, "A Comparison with Later Continental Theology."

20. Cf. Gösta Wrede, *Kyrkosynen i Einar Billings teologi* (Stockholm, 1966), pp. 56–58; also p. 7.

21. If Billing had decided to take up this problem, he would very likely have chosen an idealistic German philosophy—e.g., of the type of Rudolph Eucken. But there are many indications that Billing saw the *legitimacy* of the criticism which some of the younger philosophers in Uppsala directed against all idealistic systems of this kind.

22. This is even more remarkable because Billing chose Luther's teaching concurring *the state* as the subject of his first work.

23. Cf. Einar Billing, *Herdabrev till prästerskapet i Västerås stift* (2nd ed.; Stockholm, 1962), pp. 54 f., 65 f.

24. Cf. *De etiska tankarna*, pp. 272 f. According to Billing's presentation of Israel's development, a deterioration set in as soon as the doctrine of creation became an "independent" item. (See also *ibid.*, pp. 282–85).

25. Billing was not then able to see that Nygren and Bring preferred an attachment to Phalén rather than to Hägerström. In an article published in 1925 (*Svensk teol. kvartalskrift* [1925], p. 39), Nygren refers directly only to Hägerström. This article appeared in the very first

number of *Kvartalskrift*, and many regarded it as Nygren's declaration of his proposed program. Phalén was not mentioned.

26. Einar Billing, *Luthers lära om staten* I (Uppsala, 1900), pp. 124–37.

27. Einar Billing, *Our Calling*, rev. trans. Conrad Bergendoff ("Facet Books – Social Ethics Series," 1; Philadelphia: Fortress Press, 1964), p. 15.

28. *Ibid.*, p. 16.

29. The different view of the calling which Billing develops in *Our Calling* depends entirely on the exodus motif as applied to the individual (see pp. 39 f.).

30. See Billing's preface (1916), now included in *I katekesundervisningens tjänst* (2nd ed.; Stockholm, 1943), pp. vii–x, especially p. ix. (See also the preface by the editors [1943], *ibid.*, pp. iii f.). The most important pages in the text itself are p. 10 (on conscience), pp. 154–58 (on the outline of the subjects), pp. 41 and 213 n. 8 (on the first article).

31. See especially *ibid.*, pp. 155–57.

32. In both instances the passages are brief and easily misunderstood. Evidently Billing expresses something in 1934 which he had always, even in 1913, silently presupposed. The traditional teaching about conscience has not *one* aspect but many. And these are not always compatible.

33. See also *De etiska tankarna*, pp. 300 f. In Jesus' proclamation a unique feature enters: nature becomes the bearer of God's grace to the individual.

34. Einar Billing, "Den teologiska fakultetens ställning vid universiteten," *Vår lösen* (1912), p. 308 (italics mine).

35. Cf. Friedrich Gogarten, *Verhängnis und Hoffnung der Neuzeit* (Stuttgart, 1953), e.g., pp. 82–99, 129–43. Also K. E. Løgstrup, *Den etiske fordring* (Copenhagen, 1956), pp. 111–32.

36. See above, I.1, "Historical Criticism of the Bible," and I.2, "Free Church and State Church in Sweden."

37. *De etiska tankarna*, p. 130; cf. p. 266. Billing provided the formulation, but not on the basis of the biblical texts. The Bible also speaks of establishing boundaries, but in that context "life" is not the subject of the sentence.

# CHAPTER VIII

# CONCLUSION:

## RETURN AND RECONSIDERATION

Theology lives today in the knowledge that it has neglected something for a very long time. Just as a person with guilt feelings may throw himself into a number of activities without thereby solving his problems, so theology today is tempted to try various modern projects, especially such that receive applause. If a person lives in anxiety over that which he has neglected in the past, he needs a great deal of applause.

It is much easier for theology than for a private individual. In ordinary life there are elemental and obvious omissions for which the individual can never make amends. He cannot re-create the original situation of the offense. It is past and gone. But theology, especially by its literary production, has a field behind it in which the rectification of past mistakes can very easily be accomplished. If one then limits oneself to pointing out and correcting the mistakes in books that others have written, all that is necessary is to go to work.

This is today's situation for almost all of us who are theologians. We need to return to the situation at the end of World War I—about 1920. We need to reconsider the problems that were *then* relevant and that were not worked through but were rather set aside from the 1920's on. Since these problems were merely submerged, they still lie there, festering under the surface.

The time around 1920, when he ended his tenure as professor, was a line of demarcation for Einar Billing. These
years were also a line of demarcation for Karl Barth and
Rudolph Bultmann, men who more than anyone else have
been involved in the changing of the theological climate during the past half-century. In 1921 both commenced their
work as permanent professors, the one in Göttingen, the other
in Marburg. At the same time Anders Nygren defended his
doctoral thesis, *The Religious A Priori (Religiöst apriori),* at
Lund and began his somewhat quieter reconstruction of
Swedish theology.[1] It seldom happens that in so relatively
limited an area so much begins at the same time. It is possible
that we forget what it was that disappeared. But we, in at-
tempting here to analyze a theology that appeared before
1920, have really more reason to define what *ended.* We
must do this because that which was not permitted to continue into our own time presents the fundamental and unresolved problem for the present.

The vital issue is the *human element* in the biblical books
and in the person of Jesus. The theology which called itself
liberal, and whose glory was that against all opposition it
maintained the right of critical research into the biblical texts,
had difficulties with the divine element in the biblical word
and with the divinity of Christ. But, on the contrary, the
human feature was self-evident, natural, and unquestionable.
I have the impression that this liberal theology, which flour-
ished in Europe in the theological faculties of the universities
up to the 1920's and then began to decline, was the last
theology which had any significance for general cultural life.
To the extent that the biblical texts and the person of Jesus
strike fire outside of the confines of official churches and call
forth actions, ideals, and social concern, the source is even
today this liberal theology. But *one thing* liberal theology was
not able to do. It could not regenerate the *church.* It could not

revitalize this specific social group known as "the church." Why not? Because every form of the church lives on the administration of "the means of grace," word and sacraments. This administration presupposes that what is now "distributed" is something not merely human. That the word in the congregation is a divine word, and that Christ does God's work now through the means of grace among those who receive them, this is the *sine qua non* for the existence of the church.

No one comes to the point of accepting the word of Christ as a word from God except by a leap. Some believe it possible to show plausibility by profound research into certain human religious data that Christ and the biblical word possess some divine qualities. But that notion is one of those unbelievably naïve ideas which sometimes appear even in colleges and universities. Barth was unaffected by this narrow-minded notion. He regarded a leap as a necessary element in the faith he as a systematic theologian had to elucidate. It is understandable that he became the one who returned to the churches a measure of self-confidence that liberal theology had been unable to give. In all the churches, however, there were small groups of dejected fundamentalists who had been paralyzed by biblical criticism and who now sniffed fresh air when Barth, in about 1920, began his attack on the liberals. By themselves these enemies of historical criticism were not able to dethrone the intelligent liberalism at the universities. But supported by the giant, Barth, who at heart always despised his reactionary "friends," they dared to emerge slowly from their hiding places. During the decades between 1930 and 1950 they foisted the label "liberal" on everyone who held that the four Gospels might contain some narratives without historical foundation. This cooperation between very sophisticated Barthianism and really stupid fundamentalism, sometimes merely hypocritical, was the most fatal development of everything that started around 1920.

What ended at that time was an open, honest, and uncomplicated historical attitude toward the person of Jesus and toward the biblical material as a whole. It is true that among the older theologians Bultmann has done more than anyone else to keep alive in the churches the critical question about the biblical material. But he did this in conjunction with Heidegger's philosophy, which to many Europeans appeared as loaded with "leaps" as the Christian faith. It demands a *sacrificium intellectus* which does not differ greatly from the kerygmatic demand of obedience.

It is typical of Einar Billing that he permitted every reader to retain his probing reason intact through all the labyrinths of Christology, "the work of the Father," "forgiveness of sins," and "the vicarious death on the cross." He did not render any verdicts on all these matters except those which a critical historian would make.[2] But he nevertheless arrived at *the church and its functions*. It is true that at this point he also mentioned the mystery of the resurrection at the threshold of the church. But this leap, "the decision," to use a popular term, that this message of the resurrection expects from us, may very well wait for the moment. The gospel lies embedded in the territorial congregation, in the national church, in this "church without commitment," as it is somewhat contemptuously called nowadays. But, said Billing, this is what the church should be. Only in this way can it bear witness to mercy. There is perhaps no one but Billing who has made this aspect of the church a badge of honor. According to his conception, the church makes its clearest witness in infant baptism—in this act which, measured by the demand for a commitment, appears beautiful but meaningless.

In reality the human features of Jesus were an embarrassment not only to the crowds in the churches who were faithful to the confessions, but also to Barth himself, who sensed the difficulties. The text, "the word became flesh," could be used often, because it implied a divine action from above down to the human level. But Jesus' appeal to the Father in Gethsemane was not a very useful word in the church. He prayed that if possible he might avoid draining the cup that involved death on the cross. It was a request from a praying man to God, a partner in the conversation. The New Testament can keep these divine and human aspects together, and only when they are kept *together* does the witness to the incarnation become genuine. But the Evangelists did not have to contend with a liberal theology. They did not need to encourage a church which had lost its message because of criticism from the universities. The anti-liberal reaction after 1920 became bound by the liberals' earlier usage of the human features of the biblical record. As the texts had seemingly lost their authority because of the human element, and as the churches nevertheless needed to preach an authoritative word, they were easily driven to suppress "the human" in Jesus and in the Bible. It appears to me that Billing as a systematic theologian was unique in that his thinking was formed in the fiery furnace of biblical criticism and that he retained the marks of this experience throughout his life without ever trying to cover them up with an assumed churchly certainty.

This attitude came not to be shared by many, at least in Sweden. It began to disappear during the 1920's, and the process gained momentum after 1930. The theologians were proud of their ability to "gather" the church and to persuade even the enemies of historical criticism to come along. They learned to assume a double attitude: scholarly in their associations with the centers of learning, and ponderously churchly toward the congregations. Naturally, they did not deny the right of critical research, they just did not mention the results when the audience consisted of church people. Billing was unwilling to conform to this schizoid system of playing two roles. He was remarkably whole and honest in all of his

dealings. Every once in a while he would take up the criticisms and emendations of historical research in his sermons
and relate such matters in the presence of the congregation
at worship. He did this as bishop, and not only during his years
as professor.[3]

Einar Billing was molded in one piece without cracks. When
as a young professor he joined in the heated debate about
separating the theological faculties from the universities, his
main concern was for the church, not for his own scholarly
study. If this separation should come, *the most important
matter* would be to maintain the same free, scientific atmosphere in the free institutes for ministerial training as in the
universities. They must have this freedom for the sake of *the
gospel,* in order that in the future the proclamation might
remain genuine and faithful without timidity or falsification.[4]

A person who acts as Billing did holds the congregation in
great esteem. If one does not show such respect for the congregation, and instead tries to shield it from the dangers of
the world, one has to accept it for what it becomes—immature
and inferior. In our day, following Bonhoeffer, there is a great
deal of talk about *die mündige Welt,* "the world come of age."
Paul's words about the child who for a time is under guardians
and then later succeeds to the control of the inheritance (Gal.
4:1–7) have often been quoted in this context. But if we use
*this* word about "maturity," it is more appropriate to speak
of *the Christian congregation* rather than "the world" as a
people of mature and free persons (cf. Gal. 4:30—5:1).[5] The
modern tendency to ascribe to the "world" those Christian
functions which the New Testament ascribes to the congregation is due to the fact that the conception of the church
has first been narrowed down in a one-sided manner.

In his earlier writings Bonhoeffer appeared as an unusually
consistent Barthian. He rejected the doctrine of creation and
described the church as the sole point of contact between God

and man. The change came without a theological reconstruction and without a new and consistent theological foundation. His experience in prison and his disappointment in regard to the German confessional church's concentration on its own existence drove him to following the line which has enticed many: *von der Kirche zur Welt,* "from the church to the world." The magnetic power of martyrdom makes his appeal more potent. Instead of trying to understand the world from the point of view of the Creator and his law, the growing number of theologians of secularism interpret everything, including the world, in a christological sense on the basis of the second article of the creed.[6] What happens is that one first constructs, with the assistance of a strict demand for commitment, a narrow conception of the church. After that, one turns in bitter disappointment away from the small group and says that the world stands closer to Christ.

Einar Billing, with his open church where "decision" was never permitted to become the primary criterion and therefore also never had to be rescinded, appears almost supernaturally sensible in comparison with these violent gyrations on the European continent. There is very likely something that we can yet learn from his conception of the territorial parish. In that ethos which now unthinkingly is ascribed to the world, but which in reality is a following of Christ, there is a great deal that from the beginning should have been ascribed to the church, even in those cases where a personal and articulated confession of Christ was lacking.[7]

The view of the Bible, Christology, and the conception of the church are three areas in which present-day theology would do well to return to the statement of the problem as it was made at the end of World War I. Einar Billing was just one among those who were then shunted aside. There are others among these older authors who have long been regarded contemptuously as "liberals" by young novices but

who deserve renewed study in our time. Only a few of these
are as forgotten and as unknown outside of Sweden as Einar
Billing. But in reconsidering and rectifying this neglect we
will find that Billing has another characteristic which makes
the study of his writings fruitful. We can learn from him without having to accept him as a whole. He is at the same time
inspiring and perfectible, not least in respect to his struggle
with the Old Testament.[8] Some forms of systematic theology
are so tightly constructed that one has either to take it all or
leave the whole unused. Einar Billing's inner certainty is like
the compass needle. It points continually in one direction,
but it is also capable of movement.

NOTES TO CHAPTER VIII

1. Barth became honorary professor at Göttingen in 1921. Before
Bultmann began his teaching at Marburg in 1921, he had been professor for a year in Giessen. Nygren became associate professor
(*docent*) in Lund in 1921 and professor in 1924. Barth never produced
a doctoral dissertation, nor was he ever associate professor (*docent*).
He came directly to the university from a country parish in Switzerland.

2. See especially III.4 above, "Death and Resurrection," where the
national church also appears in the discussion.

3. See Einar Billing, *Guds närhet* (2nd ed.; Stockholm, 1949), pp.
45–49.

4. See Einar Billing, "Den teologiska fakultetens ställning vid universiteten," *Vår lösen* (1912), p. 309; cf. also pp. 319 f. His position
remained the same when he became bishop; see his *Universitet och
kyrka* (Stockholm, 1923), pp. 20–22.

5. Cf. also Friedrich Gogarten, *Verhängnis und Hoffnung der Neuzeit* (Stuttgart, 1953), pp. 31–34.

6. A very important work in this respect is Klaus Herrusdorf's unpublished master's (*licentiat*) thesis (Lund, 1961) on Bonhoeffer's
development up to 1940. See also Gustaf Aulén's critical review of
Bonhoeffer's writings in his review of *Widerstand und Ergebung*
(*Letters and Papers from Prison*) in *Svensk teol. kvartalskrift* (1962),
p. 264.

7. See the whole section IV.3 above, "The Territorial Parish and the Individual." In regard to the sudden reversal of the concepts "church" and "world," cf. Dietrich von Oppen, "The Era of the Personal," *Man in Community*, ed. Egbert de Vries (New York: Association Press, 1966), pp. 165 f.

8. The chief difficulty is Einar Billing's one-sided interpretation of the relationship between Genesis and Exodus. This interpretation influences everything: his conception of state and church, of law and gospel, of baptism, of the doctrine of the calling, of the relationship between gift and demand in the conception of the church, etc. In all the chapters of our presentation we have touched on and discussed this chief difficulty from various points of view.

# SELECTED
# BIBLIOGRAPHY

**I. Major Works by Einar Billing**

1. *Luthers lära om staten (Luther's Teaching Concerning the State)*. Academic dissertation. Part I, Uppsala, 1900. Parts II and III unpublished.

2. *Den uppriktige och Gud (The Sincere Man and God)*. Uppsala, 1904. 2nd ed.; Uppsala, 1917.

3. *De etiska tankarna i urkristendomen i deras samband med dess religiösa tro (The Ethical Thoughts of Early Christianity in the Context of Its Religious Faith)*. Uppsala, 1907. 2nd ed. enlarged; Stockholm, 1936.

4. *Försoningen (The Atonement)*. Uppsala, 1908. 2nd ed.; Stockholm, 1921.

5. *Vår kallelse (Our Calling)*. Uppsala, 1909. 5th ed.; Stockholm, 1956. Rev. Eng. trans. Conrad Bergendoff. ("Facet Books – Social Ethics Series," 1.) Philadelphia: Fortress Press, 1964.

6. *De heligas gemenskap (The Communion of Saints)*. Uppsala, 1911. 2nd ed.; Uppsala, 1919.

7. *I katekesundervisningens tjänst (In the Service of Catechetical Instruction)*. Stockholm, 1916. 2nd ed.; Stockholm, 1943.

8. *Luthers storhet (Luther's Greatness)*. Uppsala, 1917.

9. *Herdabrev till prästerskapet i Västerås stift (Pastoral Letter to the Clergy of the Diocese of Västerås).* Stockholm, 1920. 2nd ed.; Stockholm, 1962.

10. *Universitet och kyrka (The University and the Church).* Stockholm, 1923.

11. *Den svenska folkkyrkan (The Swedish National Church).* Stockholm, 1930. 2nd ed.; Stockholm, 1963.

12. *Guds närhet (God's Presence).* Posthumous. Stockholm, 1948. 2nd ed.; Stockholm, 1949.

## II. Major Articles by Einar Billing

1. "Den teologiska fakultetens ställning vid universiteten" ("The Place of the Theological Faculty in the University"), *Vår lösen* (1912).

2. "Nationellt och socialt" ("National and Social"). Unpublished. 1914.

3. "1517–1521. Ett bidrag till frågan om Luthers religiösa och teologiska utvecklingsgång" ("1517–1521. A Contribution to the Question of Luther's Religious and Theological Development"), *Uppsala universitets årsskrift* (1917).

4. "Johannes Rudbeckius' aristotelism" ("The Aristotelianism of Johannes Rudebeckius"). *Från Johannes Rudbeckius' stift.* Uppsala, 1923.

5. "Från biskop Gottfrid Billings Västeråstid" ("When Gottfrid Billing was Bishop in Västerås"), *Julbok för Västerås stift* (1925).

6. "Idealism och kristendom" ("Idealism and Christianity"). Unpublished. 1934.

# INDEXES

## I. SUBJECTS*

Agape, 150, 154
Amos, 3, 33, 67 n. 22
Anthropology, 140–42
Apocalypse of Baruch, 68, 69 n. 55, 139
Asceticism, 75–77
Atonement (*see* Work of the Father; Jesus, vicarious death; Exodus, for the individual)

Babylon, 27, 28, 43
Baptism
    ethics of, 61 f., 75 f., 112 f., 151 f.
    infant, 8, 61 f., 76, 93, 113, 151 f., 166
Baptists, 113

Call, doctrine of, 77–80, 87 f.
Catechism, Luther's, 157 f.
Chastisement of the Lord, 40–42
Church discipline, 9, 81, 132–34
Collectivism, 15, 112
Concept and event, 3, 26 f., 42 f.
"Condensed history," 26 f., 37, 40 f., 64 (*see also* Exodus, for Israel)
Confessionalism, 16 f.

Conscience, 149–53, 158
Conversion, 38 (*see also* Repentance)
Covenant, 36 f., 138 f.
Creation (*see also* Nature, Jesus' use of)
    doctrine of, 30–32, 109 f., 150–60
    groaning of, 150–52
Criticism, biblical and literary, 1–6, 14, 43 f., 135 f., 140, 164–68
Cyclical return, 29

Decalogue, 25, 157
Decision, 166, 169
Demand, 61 f., 82–84, 90, 96, 109 f., 112 f., 134 f.
Demythologizing, 57 f., 137 f.
Derailment, 36, 57, 74
Deutero-Isaiah, 31, 42, 43, 49, 66 n. 4, 67 nn. 16 & 22, 69 n. 61, 70 n. 78, 71 n. 96
Deuteronomy, 36 f., 43, 67 n. 19
Diet of Uppsala (1593), 10 f., 18, 120

*Ebed Yahweh* (servant of the Lord), 26, 44, 53

* Special attention is given in this index to subjects which are not indicated in the chapter titles of the table of contents or in the indexes of names and scripture references.

175

## II. NAMES

## III. SCRIPTURE REFERENCES

*Type,* 11 on 14 and 9 on 11 Times Roman
*Display,* Times Roman